1095

MERRITT
Lincoln MERCURY

Tales of Beaufort

Other Books by the Author

Tales of Edisto, 1955

Another Jezebel, 1958

Tales of Beaufort, 1963

Tales of Columbia, 1964

*The Amazing Marriage of Marie Eustis and
Josef Hofmann, 1965
(Co-Author)*

*The McKissicks of South Carolina, 1965
(Co-Author)*

Eliza of Wappoo, 1968

Tales of Beaufort

By

Nell S. Graydon

Illustrated with photographs

By

EUGENE B. SLOAN

Beaufort Book Shop, Inc.
Publisher

Beaufort, S. C.

First Edition 1963

Revised Second Edition 1964

Third Printing 1968

Fourth Printing 1970

Fifth Printing 1979

Copyright © 1963 by Nell S. Graydon

LIBRARY OF CONGRESS CATALOG CARD NUMBER: 63-22685

STANDARD BOOK NUMBER 910206

*Manufactured in South Carolina
By The R. L. Bryan Company
Columbia, South Carolina*
1979

TO

KATHLEEN LEWIS SLOAN

AUTHOR'S NOTE

Some history is threaded through these stories of Beaufort, but they are mostly what the title indicates—Tales.

So many old letters and diaries were destroyed when Beaufort was occupied by Union Forces—during and following the Confederate War—that it has been an almost impossible task to find recorded stories of families and experiences in the Beaufort of long ago.

The author has spent her summers for over a quarter of a century on the South Carolina coast. Through the years she has heard some of the tales. That they have varied in the telling and retelling is to be expected.

In and around Beaufort are many beautiful houses, large and small, not mentioned in this book. It has been impossible to include all of them.

"Tales of Beaufort" has been written with the earnest desire that the book will bring only pleasure to those who turn its pages.

—Nell S. Graydon.

ACKNOWLEDGMENTS

The tremendous research in "Tales of Beaufort" has been aided by many people who have told me stories, allowed me to read diaries or look through their scrapbooks at clippings and photographs, and to them I wish to express appreciation for infinite patience; also to those who so generously gave permission to photograph their homes.

For these and countless other favors, grateful acknowledgment is given to the following who helped in some way to make "Tales of Beaufort" possible: Mr. and Mrs. G. G. Dowling, Mrs. Etta C. Foster, Mrs. Estelle Heyward McMillan, Mr. and Mrs. Howard Danner, Mr. and Mrs. Joab M. Dowling.

Also, Miss Beatrice Milley, Mrs. B. F. Davis, Mr. John F. Morrall, Mr. Robert Woodward Barnwell, Mrs. Toland Sams, Mrs. Perry Sams, Mr. Jimmy Greene, the Reverend John W. Hardy, Mrs. J. E. McTeer, Mrs. F. H. Christensen, James G. Thomas, Mrs. Douglas Gregorie, Sr., Mrs. Roberta Wright.

Also, Mr. Voit Gilmore, director U. S. Travel Service, Mr. Paul Lehman, deputy director Sales Promotion Division and Mr. Will Arey, Media Relations Division, all of the United States Department of Commerce, Mrs. Katherine Drayton Mayrant Simons, president of the Poetry Society of South Carolina and Mr. Frank W. Schork, executive vice-president of the Beaufort Chamber of Commerce.

Also, Mr. Charles E. Fraser, Mrs. Edward G. Sanders, Mrs. Loulie Guerad Altmann, Mrs. A. P. Sullivan, Mr. and Mrs. Hazell Heyward, Mrs. Helen Jevons, Mr. Frank Ramsey.

Especially do I thank Mrs. Granville T. Prior of the S. C. Historical Society, Mrs. Clara Jacobs of the Caroliniana Society of the University of S. C., the personnel of the Charleston Library Society, the entire staff of the Beaufort County

Library, who by their courtesy and cooperation have helped make this book possible, Mrs. Robert Sams, Mrs. Florence H. Marhart, Miss Elizabeth Porcher, librarian, and Miss Louise Watson, also of the Greenwood County Library, Mrs. William Stuart Davies and Mrs. Eugene B. Sloan.

To Mr. Ed O'Cain of The R. L. Bryan Company my appreciation is expressed for his interest and understanding assistance in many stages of the work.

Contents

Illustrations

(x)

Illustrations

(xi)

Illustrations

Tales of Beaufort

Introduction

BEAUFORT TOWN stands proud and serene on a high bluff fronting the Beaufort River. Soft ocean breezes stir the thick foliage and the graceful drapery of gray-green moss on the huge old oaks. Palmettoes, fragrant shrubs, grass and colorful flowers grow luxuriantly between stately trees.

Days the town is bathed in golden sunshine, nights in silver moonbeams. Once in a great while, when the foghorns sound their eerie warning, and the whispering wind is still, the mist creeps in from the sea.

It spreads like a bridal veil over the sleeping town, and hovers like a benediction about the ancient spire of St. Helena, then gently touches the graves of her dead. Wisps of the gossamer-like messenger from the sea dip between buildings and lovingly caress the old walls. The mist lingers, white and ghostly on the surface of the river, then recedes before the rising sun.

There is a legend that centuries ago Beaufort was covered by water, and when the mist veils the town, the sea is reaching out and vainly trying to claim her own.

And, one cannot but feel that she has showered the town, like a favorite child, with her richest blessings. Through the blue waters to Beaufort's door, comes the bounty of the sea—the finest crabs, fish and oysters are there for the taking. No tidal wave has ever swept across the Bay to destroy historic buildings, and in time of storms, protected by her barrier islands, she has suffered less than most.

Many writers have described in prose and poetry the beauty, charm, and rich heritage of Beaufort. Many historians have pictured, step by step, the discovery in 1521 of Port Royal Island where Beaufort is located, and the arrival in 1562 of Jean Ribaut with a band of Huguenots.

They have told of the naming in 1711 of Beaufort Town, and of the arrival, through the years, of the Spaniards, Frenchmen, Indians, British and Union soldiers—all of whom, for a short time, have claimed her for their own. In minute detail, the eras have been faithfully recorded for all posterity.

This book is mostly a story of some of Beaufort's old houses, and the people who lived in them. It is a story of the nearby countryside, and some of the barrier islands. But most of all, it is a story of a way of life that is no more.

A Town's Peculiarity

BOOKS and the boats I sing:
And this old town of note,
Where each man had a library
And every man a boat.

Leisure and island homes!
For them old Homer wrote,
And oft they went to Odysseus
To learn about a boat.

They'd sit upon a balcony
With Gibbon, Hume and Grote,
And then they'd take some exercise
With six oars and a boat.

Plantations all had muscled crews,
A landing and a boat,
Each lad was taught to sail and row,
But also how to quote.

On summer morns they loved to read;
On summer eves to float,
Woe to the man who had no books
Or chanced to have no boat!

For Beaufort was a strange old town
In those old days remote:
One had to have a library;
One loved to have a boat.

Robert Woodward Barnwell

(5)

St. Helena Episcopal Church

IN an old history of St. Helena Episcopal Church there appears this charming description of the edifice:

"Enclosed in a high brick wall, it sits like an ecclesiastical poem among its grayed lichened gravestones; its slender spire piercing the green masts of the trees like a clear bugle call.

"Ancient live oaks, with their swaying banners of gray moss, weave myriad leafy designs of light and shadow to fling against its mellowed, pinkish walls of brick and tabby. When the wind blows, the palmettoes chant a requiem for those who sleep beneath the stones. The tall sycamores, green gold in autumn, silver green in spring, march two by two like loving sentinels from the East gate. . . .

"In the early spring, a purple flame creeps along the walls, creating a scene of such breathtaking beauty that artists' easels set up along the path seem almost a natural part of the scene.

"St. Helena Episcopal Church is one of the oldest as well as one of the most beautiful of the early churches in America. Built to fill the need of a struggling young colony, it is simple almost to austerity, rising four square and solid to withstand storms, wars and time, for more than two hundred years."

The old church has witnessed prosperity and adversity— she is filled with memories of joy, and sorrow. She has witnessed the heartbreak of death and parting. In her past, heavy drab caskets were often borne by faithful black hands to the altar. For generations tiny infants have been christened at her font. Young girls in gossamer white veils, and solemn little boys, have knelt at her altar for confirmation. Within her walls is Beaufort's unwritten story of birth, faith, life, war and death.

In that golden era when rice and cotton brought untold wealth to the Southland, brides in handsome satin brocade and fine handmade lace, plighted their troth within her walls. Stories are told of weddings celebrated in the old church when the gowns of the brides and their attendants came from France and cost a fortune.

Then there was war!

Soldiers of many wars have knelt with their brides at St. Helena. In the early months of 1861, men in the gray of the Confederacy walked proudly with firm tread and serious faces beside their loved ones to the altar . . . then with a hasty goodbye were off to war.

When the advanced guard of occupation invaded Beaufort in 1861, it destroyed the fine organ in St. Helena; and committed other acts of vandalism. Later the edifice was entirely disarranged and used as a hospital for Union forces. Gravestones were moved inside for operating tables.

Among the graves of St. Helena are those of a romantic figure, Elizabeth Barnwell Gough, and her daughter, Marianna, who are buried side by side.

Mrs. Gough is recalled as the builder of the Beckett House, considered one of Beaufort's loveliest. As Elizabeth Barnwell—a beauty and a belle—she accompanied her mother's brother and his wife on a voyage to England in 1772. On shipboard, Elizabeth, a granddaughter of "Tuscarora" Barnwell, met Captain Richard Gough, with whom she fell in love. Upon arriving in England, they were married, living there for some years before returning to this country. Their child, Marianna, was the wife of James Smith.

This story of one of the graves was found in the church history: Beneath a brick vault in the cemetery rest the remains of a man by the name of Perry who was so afraid of being buried alive that he is said to have instructed his family to put with him into his coffin a jug of water,

(7)

a loaf of bread and a hatchet, so that in case he came to after death, he could refresh himself while cutting his way out.

For many years the old church was without a steeple. According to Dalcho's history, the original spire rose 118 feet. In recent years the generous former owner of nearby Castle Hill plantation, John S. William, offered $10,000 for a replacement. Today St. Helena's steeple rises tall and stately above the town.

Many prominent men have served the church as rectors, six of whom became bishops. Under the wise guardianship of her beloved rector, the Reverend John W. Hardy, St. Helena Episcopal Church continues to move forward, keeping pace with the present—proud of its historic past.

The Barnwells

I

JOHN BARNWELL was born in Ireland. In 1701, at the age of thirty, he came to South Carolina and settled in Beaufort. He soon made an enviable place for himself in the province.

In 1712 the Tuscarora Indians in North Carolina conspired to exterminate all settlers in Carolina. As captain, John Barnwell commanded a body of militia and friendly Indians, and after a long, hard battle defeated the Tuscaroras.

To this day Barnwell is often referred to as "Tuscarora John" because of this successful campaign.

In 1719 Captain Barnwell was chosen by the people as agent for the province to apply to the King . . . to beseech

His Majesty to take the province under his immediate protection and release them from tyranny of the Proprietary Government. Captain Barnwell succeeded in this mission.

Captain Barnwell was a very fine map maker. Originals of his maps are treasured in London today.

II

In 1779 another Barnwell, Robert, distinguished himself at Port Royal. There Major Gardner and a detachment of two hundred men were sent by the British to take possession of the island. They were met and driven off by Major General Moultrie and an equal number of men.

In the engagement the British lost almost all their officers. Several prisoners were taken by a small group of Port Royal Militia, commanded by Captain Robert Barnwell.

The same year Barnwell was severely wounded in an enemy attack on John's Island. Dr. Johnson relates in his reminiscences that "the first sentinel, whether from fright or treachery, ran off without firing an alarm gun and saved his life; the second sentinel was James Black, ship carpenter of Beaufort. He fired his gun but was immediately bayoneted and died of his wounds.

"The Beaufort party was surrounded and commanded to surrender. Captain Barnwell called out to know what quarter they would have. 'No quarter to rebels,' was the reply.

" 'Then men,' said Captain Barnwell, 'defend yourself to the last; charge!' In an instant the click of every gun was heard as it was cocked and presented to the face of the enemy, who immediately fell back.

"Shortly after this, Sergeant of the British called 'Surrender and you shall have honorable quarter.'

" 'By what authority do you promise quarter, if we accept it—what rank do you hold?' asked Captain Barnwell.

" 'I am a Sergeant in command, but my word is as good as any officer's in His Majesty's service.'

"On this assurance, Barnwell and his men surrendered their arms and the British soldiers immediately commenced an attack on them with their bayonets, killing or wounding most of the Beaufort Company. Robert Barnwell received seventeen wounds. He was left for dead but by the kindness and attention of Mrs. Gibbs who lived on an adjoining plantation, he recovered."

Robert Barnwell, who later became Colonel, served his country in both war and peace. After the war was over, he was Speaker of the House of Representatives in the State Legislature, and a delegate to Congress from South Carolina.

Through the years descendants of "Tuscorora" have been men and women of achievement. It would take a book to list all of them and their accomplishments. Through their marriage into so many other prominent Beaufort families, it is hardly possible to find one not related by blood or marriage.

At one time there were seventeen Barnwell houses in Beaufort. How numerous they were is illustrated by a story told in the old St. Helena Church History:

"A descendant of the Barnwell family who came to visit the churchyard was impressed with the number of his relatives buried there. He remarked to the Negro sexton, 'There seems to be a lot of Barnwells here.'

" 'Yes Suh!' the sexton replied, 'de Barnwells sho been a powerful nation'."

III

BARNWELL'S CASTLE

Robert Gibbs Barnwell, grandson of Tuscarora, built a four-story house overlooking the Bay. It was so large and handsome that it became known as "The Castle." One unusual feature was that there were two front doors.

A lighted lantern on a high post in front of the house served at night as a guide to the channel for all boats coming up the river.

When Lafayette came to Beaufort in 1825, arrangements had been made for an elegant ball to be held in "The Castle." Unfortunately he was delayed, and the ball had to be held without the honor guest.

IV

Robert Woodward Barnwell was born in the big house and grew up in Beaufort. He was graduated in law from Harvard; and after practicing for a short while in his home-town, he was elected to Congress. He became President of South Carolina College and later resigned to become United States Senator. Barnwell College named for him is one of the important buildings at the University of South Carolina today.

Barnwell took an active part in the Confederate government, attended the convention at Montgomery as a delegate when Jefferson Davis was elected President of the Confederacy; and later became State Senator. After the war, he was again President of South Carolina College.

V

A young Robert W. Barnwell, Jr., was equally famous, though in a different way. He was graduated from South Carolina College at the age of nineteen, and was chosen professor of Philosophy and Sacred Literature, later becoming chaplain of the college.

While in Columbia, Robert fell in love with lovely Mary Singleton and they were married. Mrs. James Chesnut describes her in "Diary from Dixie:"

"Mrs. Robert Barnwell called. She is exquisitely beautiful, cold, quiet, calm, lady-like, and fair as a lily, but with the blackest and longest eyelashes, and her eyes so light in color that someone said 'They are the hue of cologne and water'."

The Reverend Mr. Barnwell was a pioneer in his efforts to secure help for the sick and suffering soldiers and was originator of the state hospitals during the Confederate War.

When South Carolina College was closed in June 1861, he hurried on to Manassas, and there he saw the need of hospitals along the line of defense. He worked untiringly; and Charlottesville, Virginia, was soon made the center for the reception of supplies to be distributed.

His achievements seem almost incredible—he was on call day or night. His appeals to the public were responsible for the establishment of the Hospital Aid Association. Someone asked James McIntosh, a newspaperman, who had made a study of Barnwell's life, how it was possible for one to have accomplished so much. Mr. McIntosh answered, "It was the man himself and the confidence he inspired that carried the work forward. His devotion to the sick, his tireless energy and his magnetism inspired all around him."

In the summer of 1863 Robert Barnwell contracted typhoid fever and was in a hospital in Staunton, Virginia. Mary, his wife, was in Columbia with her mother while she waited for the arrival of a new baby.

The night the baby was born, Mrs. Singleton, Mary's mother, received a telegram telling of Robert's death. While she stood at the window in the hallway wondering how she would tell her child, an old servant touched her gently. She turned, not looking at the Negress, and said, "Mr. Robert is dead."

"Little Miss, she dead, de baby, too," sobbed the woman.

Unbelievingly, Mrs. Singleton went into the room. One look at the doctor's face confirmed the sad news.

The Reverend Mr. Barnwell, his wife and baby, were buried in one grave in Columbia.

VI

Though the father, baby and mother had died, there were left four small boys, one named Robert for his father.

When the war was over the children were sent to their grandmother and grandfather in Beaufort, who bought a home on The Point, paying $2,000 for it. Here the children were reared by their grandparents and three maiden aunts, "Miss Hettie," "Miss Cattie," and "Miss Mamie."

Little Robert Barnwell was only five-years-old when his grandfather drove with him past the old Castle. There was little resemblance to the luxurious home left four years before. Half the windows were broken, some of the windows filled with old rags and papers. Negroes were living on each floor. It was a sad sight.

After Robert's grandparents' death, the aunts lived on in the home on The Point, reaching a very old age. They were greatly beloved in Beaufort.

Many amusing little stories were told about them by their relatives . . . but it might be unkind to print them.

VII

The large, beautiful home on the Bay, owned by the G. G. Dowlings, was built around 1800 by another grandson of Tuscarora, Edward Barnwell. Once it was known as "Sally Sixteen," because Barnwell's sixteenth child was born there.

After the Confederate War, the house was purchased by two families. The ladies were not congenial and the men—becoming tired of the constant bickering—had a partition built through the middle of the house. Thus was sacrificed a part of the magnificent curved stairway, but at least peace was restored between the two families.

The curve in the wall where part of the stairway was removed is visible, and marks of the former partition can be seen.

During the war, Federal officers were quartered in the house. At another time, a small, private school was operated in the drawing room.

Nearly a quarter of a century ago, Mrs. Maude O'Dell Doremus, a Beaufort woman, who gained fame as the leading lady in the New York cast of "Tobacco Road," lived there.

Some changes have been made to the house . . . "the original downstairs and upstairs' large open porches, which had extended and were reached from the dining room and the drawing room by pairs of doors, now visibly converted into windows. The slender columns, ten below and six above, were replaced by the four massive columns now seen. . . ."

VIII

Mrs. B. F. Davis, who lives in the Osborne Barnwell House on East Street, is a descendant of Major Thomas Barnwell. He was Captain and Vice Admiral of Carolina Colonial Navy and also a member of the Common House Assembly and Governor's Council.

The house in which she lives is very old and is put together with pegs. During the war it was used as a hospital and for many years was the home of Mrs. Davis' aunts, the

Misses Elizabeth and Jeanne Barnwell. The garden of the home is especially attractive. Enclosed by a wall, its beautiful shrubs and flowers form a border for the velvety green lawn.

Mrs. Davis and her sister, Mrs. Annie Barnwell Morton, who were born in Beaufort, were reared in their father's home a short distance away.

Mrs. Morton gained fame both for her prose and her poetry. She wrote for many of the popular magazines of her time, including *Godey's*, *Scott's*, *The Land We Love* and *Youth's Companion*.

Her poetry mainly concerns the war and her home. One entitled "Beaufort," begins

> "Nestling in the broad Atlantic
> Where the waves dash wild and free,
> Lies a fair and fertile island
> Like a gem upon the sea."

* * * *

Closely related to the family of Barnwells are the Elliotts, Stuarts, Rhetts, Samses, Heywards, Bulls and many others.

A relative, Dr. H. M. Stuart, is quoted as having said, "The Barnwells covered the region as the waters cover the sea."

Lafayette House

ANDREW VERDIER came to Beaufort with the little colony of French Huguenots who first settled in Purrysville. The ill-fated Jean de la Gaye of Retreat Plantation was also one of its number.

Andrew is credited with being the builder of the Lafayette House. If so, it was constructed after the middle of the eighteenth century.

General Lafayette was entertained in this house for a few hours. His name is so intimately interwoven into the history of the United States that our citizens, in greatful appreciation of his services during the Revolution, offered him every hospitality when he returned to this country on a visit in 1825, making his first stop in South Carolina at Charleston.

Residents of nearby Edisto Island and Beaufort, who were to receive him later, were disappointed that the length of the General's stay was unavoidably shortened. Both places had made elaborate preparations for his entertainment.

The festivities preceding in Charleston were so extensive that Marquis de Lafayette was delayed beyond his scheduled departure for Edisto Island. Before he reached the island, his boat was caught by the ebb tide and forced on a sand bar. There was nothing to do but wait for the flood tide to float it. Consequently he was able to spend little time on Edisto, but even these few short hours postponed his arrival in Beaufort until long after he was expected.

In Beaufort, Barnwell's Castle was being decorated ("dressed," as an old lady expressed it) for a grand ball to be given on the night of his arrival. The committee had nearly finished by two o'clock—the hour scheduled for Lafayette's landing—and the ladies all went down to the Bay to see the procession. Some of the people were gathered around the dock, others watching from balconies or private homes.

It was a gala and festive occasion. An arch of roses had been set up; and a scarlet carpet strewn with flowers led from the Bay to the steps of Mr. Verdier's home, a distance of several hundred yards. Guards with long white plumes on their hats stood on either side of the carpeted path.

After waiting until dark, the people went home. About twelve midnight, a messenger rode through the quiet streets and to the Castle's door, calling, "Lafayette is here!"

By the time the boat docked, the crowd had assembled again. All the boys in town held flaming torches in their hands, and a beautiful effect was created by the light shining on the arch and the white plumes of the guards.

The General spent only about two hours in Beaufort, but rather than disappoint those who had arranged such a cordial welcome, he came ashore and spoke to them from the Verdiers' porch. Since that time, this building has been known as Lafayette House.

Lafayette House has one of the most exquisite interiors in Beaufort. Its elaborately carved mantels, paneling and mahogany stairs are said to have come from England. Mr. Verdier's son, Mark, owned a shipping line which brought much of the material for the house from that country. A ballroom on the top floor runs the length of the house, where many social affairs were held, attended by ladies in satin and lace, gentlemen wearing ruffled vests and fine waistcoats, dancing the minuet.

Sheldon

THE HOME OF THE BULL FAMILY

STEPHEN BULL came from England to Charles Town on the frigate "Carolina," arriving soon after the settling of the province. As Lord Ashley's deputy, he was able to obtain large grants of land on St. Helena Island near Beaufort and on the Ashley River near Charles Town.

It is said that Bull assisted in selecting the site of Charles Town, and his son William did the same for Savannah.

(17)

Sixteen miles from Beaufort, Governor William Bull built a magnificent home and named it Sheldon Hall for his ancestral home in Warwickshire, England. He also built a large brick mansion on the northwest corner of Meeting and Ladson streets in Charles Town.

Sheldon Hall became noted for its elegant hospitality. Later, when Prince William's Parish Church was built near Sheldon Hall, the Bulls were large contributors. The story is told that on Sunday the entire congregation—sometimes numbering over one hundred—would be invited to Sheldon Hall for dinner, the gentry dining with Bull. Those not "socially-elect" were entertained by the overseer.

Some historians claim that the Bulls gave the land for the church—others offer proof that the widow of the second Landgrave, Edmund Bellinger, left fifty acres to the commissioners for the building of a church in 1747.

In 1756, Lieutenant Governor Bull gave a handsome communion service to the church; and aided it in many other ways. He is buried in Sheldon's graveyard. His coat-of-arms appears on the high marble crypt.

The first known official record of the name Sheldon is in the church on a seal dated 1824. Standing in ruins, today the church gives evidence of the handsome edifice that was first destroyed by British troops in 1779.

Many years later, the church was rebuilt, using as much as possible of the old walls. In 1865, during Sherman's March from Savannah to Columbia, his 15th Corps burned the fine, old church, leaving the sturdy walls standing. The church was never rebuilt; but hundreds of people gather annually now for a post-Easter service under the moss-draped live oaks surrounding the ruins.

William Bull's grandson, John, inherited a large plantation on St. Helena and Bull's Island, later known as Chisolm's and now called Coosaw. It is across a small creek from Ladies Island.

Ladies Island, legend says, was named in compliment to the women of the Bull family. Another version is that the island was called "Lady Blake Island," in honor of the wife of Joseph Blake, named Governor by the Lords Proprietors. With the passing of years, Lady Blake Island was shortened to "Lady." Still another version is that it was first called "Our Lady's" to honor the Virgin Mary.

In 1714, John Bull took his lovely English bride to his newly built home on Bull's Island. The time was late March and the orange trees surrounding the house were in full bloom. On entering her chamber, Mrs. Bull went to the open window and stood there inhaling the fragrance of the blossoms.

To her husband, she said, "How lovely it is here; and how sweet the odor of the orange blossoms!"

"Not so sweet and lovely as you," he replied, taking his wife in his arms.

Their happiness was short lived.

The year 1715 is still referred to in Beaufort and nearby places as the "Year of Tragedy." It was the time of the uprising of the Yemassee Indians. Incited by the Spaniards, they attacked Port Royal Island and entering Beaufort, murdered and destroyed.

Fortunately, many of the inhabitants of Beaufort had been forewarned and fled to Charles Town before the arrival of the Indians.

Captain John Bull left his home earlier that week, going by boat to Charles Town. No hint of the attack reached him. Returning in the afternoon, he found the island deserted, his home burned and the area strewn with the bodies of many of his slaves—scalped. Of others there was no trace —even his cattle gone. Frantically he searched every foot of the island, looking for his wife. All he ever found was a small satin slipper at the water's edge. She was never heard of again. Consumed by grief, Captain Bull became one of the most relentless and persevering foes of the Indians.

Although in later years he was again married, the memory of his first love occupied a chief place in his heart. Nineteen years after her death, in 1734, he gave St. Helena Episcopal Church a silver communion service in her memory. It is in use today.

This Your Land

FOR this your land you have shown me I feel a
     familiar love:
          Its water vistas, quiet marshes, dear sunshine, and
hymnsong of trees,
These manly, majestic trees, with Gothic moss hanging and
     swaying
Like fairytale mermaid hair, in the soft shore breeze;
And the rustling, stiff-barked palmettoes; the brown marsh
     grasses,
Brown by the blue of wide rivers and flame of great skies
Of the sunsets we saw, together, before the red moon
And all the stars, and the darkness, took over with wonderful
     arms.
Here there is grandeur, and joy, and continuing peace.
Always the tides of the ocean, the wave-break and the
     return,
Promising, giving, always. Ah, the sounds of these waters
And all the choirs of the birds . . .
For these things, not contained, given thanks for, in words,
I feel a familiar love.

                                        Edith Bannister Dowling

This poem was awarded the *South Carolina Magazine* prize of the Poetry Society of South Carolina in 1958 and is published by permission.

Born in England, Edith Bannister Dowling has lived in Beaufort for many years. Her husband, G. G. Dowling, a prominent attorney in Beaufort, is a descendant of the early settlers.

IHS

HOLY BIBLE

RELIGION FREEDOM AND TRUTH

HERE STOOD
CHARLESFORT
BUILT 1562
BY JEAN RIBAUT
FOR ADMIRAL COLIGNY
A REFUGE
FOR HUGUENOTS
AND TO THE
GLORY OF FRANCE

Marker on the southern tip of Parris Island commemorates efforts of the French government to implant a colony for the Crown. "Charlesfort" took its name from the monarch, Charles I. The marker, said to be a replica of one erected by Jean Ribaut who led the band of intrepid adventurers in the ill-fated venture, is reached through the heart of Parris Island. This basic training post for United State Marines has been a government facility since 1915.

(21)

The Barnwell-Dowling House on the Bay in Beaufort, now owned by Mr. and Mrs. G. G. Dowling, was built by Edward Barnwell, a grandson of Tuscarora Barnwell. The home was formerly owned by Miss Maude Odell, the famous actress, who took a leading part in the Broadway stage play, "Tobacco Road," and later was the residence of the J. E. McTeers.

The Chase House, three stories high, fronts on Beaufort Bay. The property of Mrs. Charles Luther, it is presently arranged into several roomy and attractive apartments. It is a former residence of Colonel D. C. Wilson.

Barnwell's Castle as it appeared in 1864. The four-story structure, with high basement, is no longer in existence, the present Beaufort County Courthouse standing on the site. The house was built by Edward Gibbs Barnwell before 1801. It was used as Hospital No. 5 for Union Soldiers; and from 1872-1881 dominated the square as the seat of county government. Two brothers lived here and the house had two front doors—a 19th century version of a duplex.

Negroes in parlor, Barnwell Castle, 1862. (From Harpers Magazine, 1862.)

(23)

The McKee House was built by Henry McKee for his young bride prior to the Confederate War. Due to the reversal of McKee's fortunes, and the freeing of slaves, the house was taken over by Negro Robert Smalls, a former servant in the household, who, according to his own statement, purchased it for a very low price. Smalls, a pilot of the Confederate Ship Planter, sailed her out of Charleston harbor, surrendering the vessel to the Federals. Smalls served in Congress as a Republican from South Carolina after the war; and later was appointed Collector of the Port of Beaufort. The house was recently purchased by the Charles Barnums.

At time of photograph, the home built by Colonel Means was the residence of H. P. Schwartz. Hospital No. 2 was set up in its spacious rooms for soldiers during the Confederate War.

The Means-Tucker House was built on "The Point" in the early 1850's. The large, brick structure has graceful semi-circular outside steps and portico. One side has a double veranda supported by many columns and is edged with delicate balustrade. The interior has a winding and almost free-standing stairway rising from spacious center hall.

The Episcopal Church of the Cross at Bluffton, said to be the prettiest and most unique church building in South Carolina, has been photographed many times for national publications. Original plans called for towers and a vestibule but these were never completed. According to one source, it was designed by a French architect named Dimmick, who chose black cypress for its exterior, and a fan motif of Palmetto fronds for the arch of the windows. On sunny days, a rosy glow is emitted from the pink glass of the windows. The building, having celebrated the centennial of its use in 1954, grows lovelier through the years, the cypress taking on added sheen, and the oaks of its canopy becoming statelier and more enormous.

The lovely L. A. Hall home was built in the 1840's by George Elliott and was next owned by Dr. W. J. Jenkins. After the Confederate War, it was purchased by George Holmes. The house is distinguished by its lavish interior and large Greek columns.

The Elliott House was used as U. S. Hospital No. 15 during the Confederate War. Note fire engine in foreground.

The Lafayette House is so-called because General Lafayette was entertained here in 1825 and spoke from the balcony porch to Beaufort citizens. Original photograph was made in 1862, while the house was Headquarters' offices (1861-1863) for Federal forces under command of General Stevens. General W. T. Sherman spent one day at the Lafayette House. The building today houses the offices of the Historical Society of Beaufort.

Home of Captain George Heyward at Bluffton, owned by Mr. and Mrs. Hazell Heyward.

One of the DeSaussure Houses.

St. Helena Episcopal Church has been a bellwether for Beaufort, prosperous or in decline as the fortunes of the Parish. St. Helena Parish was established in 1712; and the church building, erected in 1724, has twice since been enlarged. Of brick construction, it is finished on the outside with pink stucco. Its interior features elaborate cornices, shutters, a gallery, and simple columns ranging above the pews.

Recent photograph of entrance to Secession House shows its beautiful marble steps and iron grill work. One of the Rhett houses, it was occupied by Federal troops during the Confederate War and also the United States Tax Commissioner. Succession of owners include Mittar Maxcy Rhett, Middleton Elliott, Mae E. Barnwell, Ira Smith and Alva Carr. It is now the Claude McLeod House.

Federal officers stand on portico and in yard of occupied Secession House. The walled-in garden at rear of the house contained numerous orange trees.

The home of Mrs. Etta C. Foster.

This home, one of the more impressive in Beaufort with its huge brown columns and expansive lawn overdraped with moss, was built in 1850 by Dr. Berners Barnwell Sams as a town house. In its rear are one-room slave quarters, centered by a carriage house, all enclosed with a high wall. For years it has been known as the Crofut-Waterhouse home, and is now owned by Mr. and Mrs. Edward G. Herendeen. Mrs. Herendeen is the granddaughter of George A. Crofut who bought the house in 1896.

The same impressive facade of the Sams House with massive pillars and balcony is presented as it appeared during the Confederate War. The oaks on either side have now grown to huge proportions and become filled with Spanish moss. During the war, it was Hospital No. 8.

The Arsenal houses the Beaufort Museum whose relics date from 1711. The fortress, surrounded by high brick wall, guarded by graceful palmettoes, was erected on the foundation of the first built in 1780.

Sara Hazzard Elliott was married May 18, 1808, at Walnut Hill plantation to Richard W. Habersham, a lawyer. He built his bride this house on the Bay, with a garden stretching down to the water, landscaped with rare shrubs and flowers. On one side was a rose garden with over one hundred plants. The Habersham House, sometimes referred to as the "Pink House," was one of the showplaces of Beaufort. It was later owned by the Sanders family and its last residential owner was Miss Jennie Sanders.

The Habersham House today is Belk-Simpson Department Store.

Confiscated during the War, the Sams House was used as Contraband Hospital No. 10 (whose numbers are still visible on the upstairs' bedroom doors). The land was originally granted to Wm. deVeaux and has been owned in turn by Cuthbert, B. B. Sams (1818), M. M. Sams, M.D. (1855), B. B. Sams (1867) and A. R. Sams (1928). This house was built in 1818 by B. B. Sams and it is believed to be the only antebellum home in Beaufort to have been owned continuously by the family of the builder. Negroes are shown on porch.

The Fraser-Matteson House is now the home of Dr. and Mrs. Maurice Matteson. It was built in 1804 and is in the Adam style. Old records in the South Carolina Historical Society in Charleston contain a receipt signed by the Collector of Revenue, 3rd District Survey 1, of South Carolina, for payment of duty. The receipt says, "This is to certify that Captain Fred Fraser of the Parish of Beaufort and District S. C., hath paid the duty of $25.00 upon two two-wheel carriage and chaise owned by him, having one top to be drawn by one horse for the conveyance of person for the year and to the end of 30th of September 1801, being full amount of five years' taxes on his carriage."

Shrimp dock on Village Creek, St. Helena Island.

Retreat Plantation

ORE than a decade before the middle of the eighteenth century, Colonel Jean Pierre Purry with a small band of German, Swiss and French came to Carolina. They settled on the Savannah River and began to clear land for a town to be called Purrysburg.

Purry's little colony was mostly composed of well-to-do farmers, who had dreams of becoming wealthier in this new country. Some planned to raise rice or indigo on the fertile land, others to grow grapes to make into wine for export.

The men were industrious and ambitious, but they were unable to cope with the climate. Some contracted fever; others, unable to endure the sweltering heat, aggravated by insects that swarmed out of the thick woods and swamps, sickened and died.

Discouraged by failure, a small group of the Swiss and French emigrants moved to Beaufort. Among these was a young vintner, Jean de la Gaye—a slender handsome Frenchman, cultured and well educated, with a fortune of his own. Some thought he was a political exile.

Soon after his arrival in Beaufort he met lovely, vivacious sixteen-year-old Catherine Gautier. Her gracious manner and gentle wit endeared her to all who knew her.

She and Jean de la Gaye fell deeply in love and were married in Beaufort April 17, 1737.

Six miles from Beaufort, he bought several hundred acres of land, bounded on two sides by Battery Creek. Close to the water he erected a beautiful little house that had all the charm of a miniature French villa.

Each day, during its construction, he spent at the site. From morning 'til night, he watched the workmen mix water, lime and oyster shells, and build the walls of tabby. When completed, the walls measured twenty-two inches in width. At the same time, bricks for the chimneys were baked in a nearby kiln. The lighter ones were carefully arranged in a diamond shape as the chimneys were built.

When the structure was completed, Jean looked at it with pride. "Here," he said to Catherine, "our children and grandchildren will live. I'm building it, Ma Chère, to last forever."

Broad acres were cleared and spaded. And row after row of grape plants set out.

Beautiful furniture arrived from his old home in France. Exotic shrubs and flowers were planted on the grounds. Everything was so perfect that it was like a bit of fairyland.

The Gayes were very happy, the vineyards were productive and the years slipped by like a phantom crowd. Often Catherine rode with him through the vineyards. Evenings were usually spent singing old French songs, as she played on the harp. Their love seemed to grow stronger with time. Only one sorrow marred their lives—there were no babies to brighten the home.

Late one afternoon, Jean de la Gaye had been riding over his plantation. When he was nearly home, a servant came running to meet him.

"Come quick, Massa," she screamed, wringing her hands.

"What is the matter?"

"It's little Missie."

Without another word the startled man went rapidly to the house.

Catherine, scarcely breathing, lay upon the bed. One glance at her pale face told him that she had been stricken with the deadly fever that had taken the lives of so many of the colonists.

He immediately sent a man on a swift horse for a doctor. When the doctor arrived, Catherine was dead.

Giving instructions for the plantation carpenter to make a coffin, Jean went into the room with Catherine and closed the door. What passed within when he was left alone with his beloved, no one ever knew. But servants passing softly by the door reported hearing heart-rending sobs.

Toward morning he called for the coffin, and when it was brought into the house, he jerked a heavy silken drapery from the window and folded it into the box. He allowed no other hands to touch her; but gathering her up in his arms, placed her on the silken bed.

As the rising sun broke through the clouds and shimmered over the waters of Battery Creek, Jean de la Gaye grimly watched two stalwart black men dig a grave under the palmettoes near the front of the house. Into this was lowered the mortal remains of her he'd loved so well.

Although Jean de la Gaye had purchased a pew in St. Helena Episcopal Church, "served as a vestryman and warden, and provided the sacramental wine," no service was held.

For five years afterwards, he spent most of his time in Charles Town, returning to his plantation only when business made it necessary.

He became a miserable, haunted man who never smiled. There was little resemblance in the morose, unfriendly person to the former charming Jean de la Gaye.

On taking up his residence again near Beaufort, he became a recluse and seldom entered the town. Strange tales, that made one shudder to hear, of cruelty to servants, began to seep out from the plantation.

It was known the Frenchman was wealthy; but with the passing years his reputation as a miser grew. Broadcloth and fine linen gave way to patched homespun.

One morning a frightened Negro from Retreat Plantation appeared in Beaufort. "Massa, he dead," the man cried over and over. Authorities investigated; it was true—the owner of Retreat had been murdered by two of his slaves.

Jean de la Gaye left no will; and the plantation was sold at auction to Stephen Bull. He gave the property to his son-in-law, John Gibbs Barnwell. It remained in possession of his heirs until the Confederate War when the United States Government confiscated it.

After the war was over, the family returned to Beaufort. John Barnwell, Jr., met his brother-in-law, Edward Tabb Walker, who had married Ann Bull Barnwell, and told him of "paying the taxes for the war years and buying in Retreat for $8.00. He offered it to Walker for the same price. The latter took title and later presented it to his wife."

It has been said that a baby girl of the Walkers is "buried at Retreat under the Palmetto palms in front of the house slightly to the west." Possibly near the resting place of Catherine de la Gaye.

In the following years, various tenants lived in the old house—but not for long. Retreat acquired the reputation of being haunted; and became a rendezvous for rattlesnakes— so that it was avoided by credulous persons.

One of the stories was that on stormy nights a quaintly dressed man and woman could be seen by the glow of vivid lightning walking hand in hand along Battery Creek. Then they would turn and go toward the house. As they neared the entrance, the whiteness of the woman's gown faded away, leaving only darkness. Almost at once the music of a harp could be heard, mingling with the wild cacophony of the storm. The sound would rise, then end abruptly on a crashing discord and all would be still except for the occasional burst of thunder.

Retreat was one of the few places no tenant wished to occupy. So the years passed and the old house stood empty— like the later life of its builder. A wilderness grew around it. Children avoided it. Even scoffers kept their distance at night. Rats and squirrels scampered through the rooms. Birds built their nests in the old camellia bushes; and rabbits, raccoons and o'possums raised their young in the heavy growth.

All that is passed. Today the garden blooms with its former beauty. The exquisitely restored house stands as of yore—tranquil and lovely under the warm southern sun. No voices or footsteps haunt the occupants. It is as if the spirit of the builder, satisfied with those who sleep within the ancient walls, is at peace.

The house is owned by Antonio Ponvert of Oyster Bay, New York.

The Stuarts, Heywards, and Elliotts

THE STUARTS

IN the latter part of the eighteenth century, Francis Stuart settled in Beaufort. He became a wealthy planter and merchant. The house on Bay, where his mercantile business was located, witnessed the first celebration of the Fourth of July.

Francis Stuart and his wife, Anne Reeve, had one son, Dr. James Stuart, who married Anne Middleton.

Their descendants have lived in Beaufort through many generations.

Dr. Henry M. Stuart was known throughout the District as "Dr. Hal." Before the war, he and William Elliot spent many wonderful hours fishing and hunting. Like Elliott, he loved Beaufort and "had intense pride in it."

During the war, Dr. Stuart served with the Beaufort Artillery, afterward returning home to take up his practice. Many Union men were still in Beaufort, some ill and dying of malaria, a baffling disease to the Northerners who were unaccustomed to its symptoms.

When Dr. Stuart took charge of the sick, it is told that they "watched him narrowly, thinking he would be pleased to kill off a few Yankees," but his patients got well and suspicion was allayed.

A son, named for his father, and like him called "Hal," was one of the most beloved men who ever lived in Beaufort. It is also said that he was a very handsome man, tall and distinguished looking.

Tradition says his love for his wife and hers for him was a delightful thing worthy of any age. Hal Stuart, full of fun but also of a serious nature, loved to write about the outdoors, trees, birds, flowers. His faith was wondrous to see. On a Christmas card to friends, he wrote:

> "Hark! from yonder belfries height
> Ye Christmas Bells are ringing,
> Before ye altar's holy light
> Ye choir is sweetly singing
> And ere how sweet it sounds to me
> Christus Natus Hodie
> Christ is born today . . ."

John A. Stuart, who lived for many years on the Bay in the home built by Dr. Stoney, became the editor of *The Charleston Mercury*.

Stuart and Richard Yeadon, editor of *The News and Courier*, were good friends. Yeadon went away on vacation, and—as editors often do—wrote back long letters to his paper describing his visit. Day after day his letters appeared in the *Courier*.

These prompted Stuart to write in his *Mercury*, "Did you ever see wharves between that queer old thing, the mud machine, bringing up nothing but mud, mud, mud, mud? Just so, the *Courier* every day is laden with nothing but Yeadon, Yeadon, Yeadon, seven more Yeadons!" The piece was the town talk and the source of much laughter.

When Mr. Yeadon returned to Charleston and saw the article, he was furious. A friend went into the *Mercury* office and told Stuart that Yeadon had been walking up and down the street for an hour carrying a stick, "mad as a bull about that piece of yours."

John Stuart reached for his hat, saying, "Well, I believe I'll go down and see him." When he reached the doorway, Yeadon was coming toward him. Stuart held up his hand in greeting, saying "Good morning Dick, how are you? What's the matter? I hear you're looking for me with a stick. What's up?"

"The truth is, Stuart, I intended to give you a beating. But I've changed my mind," and Yeadon turned and went toward his office.

The subject was never mentioned again and apparently their friendship did not suffer from the affair.

When the last duel in Beaufort was fought, Mr. Stuart loaned a fine pair of silver inlaid dueling pistols to the participants. Both were killed. Stuart carried the pistols to the Bluff and threw them into the river.

THE HEYWARDS

Daniel Heyward was born early in the eighteenth century. His plantation, "White Hall," not far from Hazzard Creek, near Bluffton, was one of the first in South Carolina to produce rice in large quantities. Descendants living today remember the double line of magnificent oaks forming the semi-circular driveway to the big house.

He bought additional land on the Combahee River, cleared the swamps along its banks and began the building of a rice dynasty that was to make his son, Nathaniel, one of the wealthiest men in the state.

Nathaniel Heyward, who owned the building in Beaufort later known as the "Sea Island Hotel," inherited from his father hundreds of acres on the Combahee. Gradually he increased his holdings, and by 1850 he had added several other large plantations to "Combahee." Large numbers of laborers were required to cultivate the rice fields, so Heyward became the owner of nine hundred and ninety-nine slaves.

He died at his Combahee plantation in 1851. There he had lived for over half a century and at his request was buried in his rose garden on the plantation.

More than a decade later on May 3, 1863, a young soldier, Wallis Blake, wrote to his mother from "Combahee:"

"The Yankees came up to 'Combahee' Ferry yesterday and broke up the pontoon bridge—burning all the houses up to that point. They carried away all the Negroes from Newport and from William Heyward's place and burned the dwelling."

The home was rebuilt by the Heywards after the war and "Combahee" remained in their possession until 1911 when it was sold by Duncan Clinch Heyward, a former governor of South Carolina.

Since 1946 the plantation has been owned by Mr. and Mrs. Reamer Y. Lane.

Thomas Heyward, Jr., one of the signers of the Declaration of Independence, built his home "Old House" on a part of his father's plantation. Unlike his brother Nathaniel, he was not especially interested in rice planting—his mind was centered on law and government.

In addition to "Old House," he owned a large brick dwelling at 87 Church Street in Charleston, where his family spent several months of each year. When George Washington visited Charleston, rather than cause hard feelings among his friends by staying with any one of them, he stayed at the Heyward house which was rented for him. Since that time, the building has been known as the Heyward-Washington House.

General Washington wished to break the trip from Charleston to Savannah by spending a night with his intimate friend, Thomas Heyward, Jr., but he feared that such a plan would offend Charles Cotesworth Pinckney if he did not visit him, also. Therefore, it was quietly arranged that the general's carriage would "break down" by the gates of "Old House." Naturally, while repairs were being made, the President rested at the Heywards'.

Many members of the Heyward family from Beaufort and the plantations had summer homes on the May River at the little village of Bluffton, and spent some months of the summer there. "Mills' Atlas" in 1825 gives the name of this village as "Kirk's Bluff."

Tradition says that the first Kirks settled on the Bluff before 1800; later the Popes bought land and settled nearby. As the Heywards, Stoneys, Pritchards, Verdiers, Draytons, Coles, Baynards, Porchers, Mellichamps, Stuarts, Grahams, and additionl families came, a rivalry developed among the original settlers—each wanting the place to be called by his name. Finally, all compromised by naming it "Bluffton."

The beautiful "Church of the Cross," around which so much of the life of Bluffton has been centered for over a hundred years, was built in 1854. It stands in the shape of a cross, on a high bluff, overlooking the May River.

There has been some discussion concerning the identity of the architect of the edifice. Some claim Edward Bricknell White designed it (and there is a record that the plans he submitted were accepted by the vestry and Building Committee). But others stated that these were not used; and that a Frenchman, Dimmick, was the architect of the church and also the old Kirk home, "Roselands," once known as "Kirk's Folly." Both structures are Gothic style.

One story is that the church and house were not burned during the Yankee Invasion because a Federal officer, who was a friend of Dimmick, found them too lovely to destroy.

The late James Henry Rice, Jr., described Bluffton as "retaining enough flavor of the old days to let one know he is within the pale, surrounded by the purple-born, who through storm and stress, war and misfortune, have clung tenaciously to their birthright."

Save for the interlude of war, Heywards have had homes in Bluffton. Captain George C. Heyward returned there to live after the Confederate War. Early one morning in 1868, he went to his son's home, Buckingham Plantation, just across the river from Hilton Head. Leaving before sundown for Bluffton, he stopped at the wild turkey traps on the plantation, and an unseen assassin shot him. His murderer was never brought to justice, although an enraged District— where he was greatly respected and loved—made every effort to find the guilty party. In Alabama, many years later, an old soldier, on his deathbed, confessed the killing, in revenge for a reprimand given to him during the war by Captain Heyward.

A story is told of a stranger in Beaufort stopping a small boy on the street and asking his name. The little fellow (now a young lawyer) answered proudly, "Sir, my name is Thomas Declaration of Independence Heyward!"

One of the Heyward women, who spent her childhood in Bluffton, wrote a description of life in Bluffton and on the plantation:

"In the days before the war when splendor was in its glory and hoop skirts and tall silk hats held sway, the village was a place of wealth.

"In those days of ease and happiness, families on surrounding plantations lived in palatial homes—homes marked by beauty and culture, for they were owned by the aristocrats of the coastal regions. The planters and politicians of that time held a station in the social life of the deep South corresponding to that of royalty in the Old Country.

"Southern Colonial architecture stood out in prominence. There were spiral staircases, elegant furnishings, wine cellars, etc., with servants to command.

"Life and gaiety, old-time formalities and customs ran high. 'Marsuh' and 'Missus' sat in dignity while young sideburn 'Masters' courted young 'Missuses' in bonnets and curls. Tight-waisted, hoop-skirted figures danced and flirted in innocence and mirth."

Tradition says that Bluffton was a boiling political center during the unsettled years before the war. It is claimed that the very first secession movement in South Carolina was started on Bluffton when Dr. Daniel Hamilton delivered his famous speech under the venerable oak that to this day is called "Secession Oak."

Dr. Hamilton was visiting at the plantation home of the late M. A. Verdier family who owned "Marshlands" in Beaufort.

Later the Bluffton Movement in Secession—as it came to be spoken of—was again promoted by Barnwell Rhett, who had a summer home in Bluffton. On July 31, 1844, Rhett launched the Bluffton Movement for a State Convention. Everywhere his appeal was the same: "I proclaim to you, if you value your rights, you must resist and submit not."

Heywards continue to live in charming old Bluffton, each generation leaving a proud heritage for those who follow.

THE ELLIOTTS

In Ramsay's History, published in 1809, he, writing of Beaufort and the Elliotts said, "A causeway and ferry has been lately completed which renders the communication between the island and Main, safe and convenient. In 1795, a company of one hundred persons was incorporated for the purpose, but after expending much money and labor in trying to effect the object for near ten years they gave up the completion of it to William Elliott, who soon finished the work.

"The former company began the causeway on the island side and made it of pine logs filled in with mud, but the worms below and the influence of the weather alone was continually rendering their work nugatory. There were too many persons to consult—their deliberations were slow and their efforts feeble.

"William Elliott, at length, undertook it and began the causeway on the Main side which he finished entirely of fascines; and he had begun to face the old pine logwork in the same manner when his valuable life was terminated with the universal regret of the whole community. There is now an excellent rope ferry.

"The length of the causeway, for there is one on each side, and of the ferry, exceeds a mile. The celerity with which this work was finished by Mr. Elliott proves that in public works one head is better than many, and that causeways may be made in Carolina more easily, and with less expense than had been commonly supposed."

Since this time the Elliotts have been prominent in Beaufort, the State, and elsewhere.

* * * *

A letter from Mrs. Manigault in Philadelphia, written in 1818 to her daughter, Mrs. Lewis Morris, in Charleston, says, "We have heard great compliments of young Mrs. William Elliott. Witt says he thinks her the most beautiful woman he ever saw."

One, Stephen Elliott, born in Beaufort in 1771 and educated at Yale, was a famous Botanist. Stephen Elliott, II, was born in 1806 and became an Episcopal bishop in Georgia, while another, Robert, became a bishop in Texas.

Like the Barnwells, from whom they were descended, it would take a genealogist to keep the separate ones in order. In every Barnwell family there were a "Robert and Elizabeth," while in the Elliotts can be found "William and Stephen." Sometimes within one generation, cousins would bear identical names.

The Elliotts owned plantations on the nearby islands and rivers. They also had large town houses in Beaufort.

Many members of the Elliott family were interested in the sports of fishing and hunting. In 1859, William Elliott tells in his book "Carolina Sports" of a deer stand, erected by an ancestor, Colonel Barnard Elliott:

"The traveler in South Carolina, who passes along the road between the Ashepoo and Combahee Rivers will be struck by the appearance of two lofty white columns rising among the pines that skirt the road. They are the only survivors of eight which supported in times anterior to our Revolutionary War, a sylvan temple, erected by a gentleman, who, to the higher qualities of the devoted patriot, united the taste and liberality of the sportsman. The spot was admirably chosen, being on the bow of a piney ridge which slopes away at a long gun-shot's length into a thick swamp; and many a deer has, in times past, been shot from the temple when it stood in its pride—as we ourselves have struck them from its ruin."

William Elliott's stories of hunting and fishing were published in the best sporting magazines of the time. His tale of "Incidents of Devil-fishing in St. Helena Sound" is a rare story that every fisherman who reads it, enjoys.

Mr. Elliott also tells a tale of a phantom Buck. It all began when one of a group of hunters apparently hit a deer, so that the shot severed its leg. He records the conversation afterward:

" '. . . his seeming to be shot, yet moving as if unhurt— his losing a leg, yet running off without it—his bloodlessness; and his disappearance at May's Folly—the confusion of the hounds—and the unaccountable dispersion of the pack!—impress upon my mind the possibility of this being no deer of flesh and blood, but the Spectre Buck of which we have heard traditionally and which I never supposed had been met by daylight.'"

" 'The tradition!—the tradition!' cried several voices impatiently."

" 'It is simple enough,' I rejoined."

" 'Some forty or fifty years ago, there lived in this region, then thinly settled, a German named May. He constructed, we are told, those embankments (just at the place where we so mysteriously lost our dogs today) of which the remains are yet visible; and which were intended to reclaim those extensive marshes from waste. They failed of their purpose—involving him in pecuniary difficulty; and hence the name of 'May's Folly' which the spot still bears. He became a soured and discontented man; sometimes hunting the deer on these grounds that we have traversed today, with desperate energy, as if he would exterminate the very race—and then relapsing into a moody restlessness.

" 'He grew still more unsocial as he advanced in life, and men began to whisper strange stories of him . . . he withdrew himself more and more from the public observation . . . until at last he died.

" 'Then, it is said, that a few of his confidential slaves, to whom he had imparted his desire, complied with his dying injunctions, which were: to bury his body secretly in the midst of these wild and melancholy barrens; to level the grave and strow it over with leaves, so that no man might discover the place of his burial.

" '. . . The Negroes look on this as haunted ground; and hurry over it after nightfall, with quickened steps and palpitating heart. Sometimes a gush of air, warm as from a furnace, passes fitfully across his face, while a cold shivering seizes his frame.

" 'Sometimes a milk white buck is seen, by glimpses of the moon, taking gigantic leaps; then shrouded in a mist wreath and changed in a twinkling into a pale old man, swathed in his death clothes—then melting away slowly into air.

" 'At other times the *Spectre Buck* starts up before his eyes, pursued by phantom hounds which rush maddeningly through the glades—yet utter no sound, nor shake the leaves . . . It is the ghost of May, doing penance for the sins done in the flesh, under the form of the animal whom he most persecuted when living'."

When Mr. Elliott finished the tale (according to the book), the hunters entered into quite a discussion on the pros and cons of ghosts.

The dogs were found the next day . . . far from "May's Folly."

Another Stephen Elliott served gloriously in the Confederate War. He and a cousin, Tom, the son of William of "Carolina Sports," saw service under General Drayton.

Captain Stephen Elliot (later General) was wounded at Camp Beauregard but kept at his post until the guns of the enemy ceased. He led many a raiding party on Hilton Head after it was taken over by the Yankees—destroying anything that might be of value to the enemy. It is told that in one night he fired fourteen plantation houses on Hilton Head.

General Stephen Elliott, brave soldier and gentleman of the Old South, has left a record equalled by few men.

The Temple of the Sun

THE Hepworth-Pringle House, according to old records, dates between 1717 and 1722. Thomas Hepworth, the builder, was one of the Chief Justices of the colony and also a large plantation owner.

With the passing years the house changed owners several times. Edward Barnwell (who in 1800 built the house on the Bay once called "Sally Sixteen") is thought to have been born in this house. But before it was bought by his father, Nathaniel Barnwell, it had been owned by Thomas Burton and William De Veaux.

The house is now owned by Mr. and Mrs. Somers B. Pringle.

A traditional story is that during the Revolution, while the house was owned by John Johnson, a British gunboat was anchored in the Beaufort River, and fired from a cannon the only shot that hit Beaufort. Mrs. Johnson was in the house at the time and the shot passed over her head "killing a horse near the site of the present Baptist Church."

Another story is of the Johnsons' daughter, Margaret, or Peggy—as she was called by her family. When Peggy heard that the local Masonic Order was to hold an initiation ceremony at her father's house (where the meetings were conducted), the girl in a spirit of mischief and curiosity hid in a closet. While Peggy was a very small size, the closet, too, was little, and during the rites she made a noise while moving from her cramped position, and was discovered.

She was immediately inducted into the Order and became the one member of the Eastern Star in Beaufort. It is thought that through its association with the Masons the house was sometimes referred to as "The Temple of the Sun," although another version is that the name was derived "because as originally built, the house had a porch across the eastern end." The first version, however, seems the more logical.

After the Revolution, Sara Johnson married William Fickling who conducted a private school for boys in their home. Peggy married John McKee who built a home for her across the street from her father's.

An article in the Beaufort Library, copied from Dr. John A. Johnson's "Beaufort and the Sea Islands," appeared in the *Beaufort Republican* in 1873. It relates "At the close of the last century, an early cotton gin was invented and the first one exhibited in our parish was set up in the large front parlor of the Dutch-looking building at the southwest corner of New and Fort Republic streets—to the 'Moderns,' known as 'Republican Headquarters'."

Like many of the old houses in Beaufort the Hepworth-Pringle house has a tabby foundation and is "so built with long piercings in the thick wall that muskets can be aimed in either direction; underneath the openings there runs a ledge on which munitions could be stored."

Behind the brick wall, to the left of the entrance, Mrs. Pringle has developed a strikingly attractive garden of ornamental shrubs, roses, azaleas, camellias and perennials.

Riverview

1710

THE Hext-Morris House sits on a curve beside the Beaufort River, on what is locally known as "The Point." In the late seventeen hundreds it was the plantation home of Elizabeth Hext Sams. At this time it was separated from Beaufort by water and was not a part of Beaufort Town, but on Black's Island, and surrounded on three sides by tall pines. After Elizabeth Hext married William Sams, it became known as Sams Point.

The house is built on a high basement of tabby. At the rear, the Beaufort River stretches between it and Ladies Island, therefore the present owner has called it, "Riverview."

Riverview has the simplicity of very old houses. Many of the windows have their original, tiny panes, with as many as six in the upper sash and nine below. The heavy, low doors are equipped with old "H" hinges. The beams were cut from first-growth pine, as was the sheathing and wide board floors. The walls of the halls and bedrooms are of smooth, vertical planks with wide joints.

The staircase in the rear reception hall is a masterpiece of the joiner's art, put together with wooden pegs and hand-cut nails.

Large shade trees, white oleanders and palmettoes, grow in the spacious yard, enclosed by a picket fence. Camellias and azaleas bloom in a formal, brickwalled garden on the east and west sides of the house.

Mrs. Irma H. Morris owns Riverview and has an antique shop in her home, filled with rare eighteenth century pieces.

This house—as very old houses should—has its ghost story, too. When Mrs. Morris bought it, an old Negro was her gardener. She noticed that often he would spade deep holes over the yard, for no apparent reason. Finally she asked "Why aren't you working the flower beds instead of wasting your time?"

"I no waste time, Missus, I'se looking for gold."

"Looking for gold? You're searching in a strange place!"

"No'm, de funny men told me it here."

On questioning him further, Mrs. Morris was told that people in clothes that he had never seen "the like of" came to him at night; he accurately described them in the dress of two hundred years before. Then he said "they" had promised to show him where they had buried a pot of gold on Sams Point.

One morning, soon after daybreak, Mrs. Morris was awakened by a loud knocking. A little provoked when she opened the door and saw the old Negro standing there, she said, "This is too early to start work."

"Tonight's the time, Missus. I couldn't sleep. They'se goin' let me see the gold tonight!"

The following morning, the old Negro did not show up, and Mrs. Morris went to his home to see if he was in any trouble. She was much perturbed when she found that during the night he had suffered a stroke and was speechless! He died soon afterwards.

One wonders if, as the time drew nearer for the event he had dreamed of for so long, the excitement was too much for the old fellow, causing his fatal illness.

For many years the old Hext place has had the reputation of being "haunted." Undoubtedly pirates between 1700-1710 landed on the nearby barrier islands and they also probably hid in the thick pines of the plantation on The Point, burying their stolen treasure there.

The Anchorage

THE Anchorage, on the Bay, is one of Beaufort's oldest and most impressive houses. The three and one-half story mansion was built by William Elliott and was the scene of many important political and social gatherings in that golden era before the Confederate War. Federal officers occupied the house after Beaufort was invaded.

Later it was occupied by the exclusive Ribaut Club who counted among its members officers of various ships touching port. Like a miniature Monte Carlo, the club was complete with bar, roulette wheel and numerous other gambling devices. It was a far cry from the gracious, cultured people whose home it had been for generations.

For a time, The Anchorage served as an annex to the Sea Island Hotel; and during Reconstruction days when Wade Hampton was waging his bitter political campaign, a northern woman wrote of hearing him speak from its porch.

Admiral Beardsley, a graduate of the Naval Academy, came to Beaufort as commandant at Parris Island. He admired the place and on retirement purchased it. It is said that the old house acquired its name "Anchorage" from the sea-minded owner.

Admiral Beardsley and his wealthy wife, a daughter of a banker in Little Falls, New York, spent $80,000 remodeling. Changes were made on the exterior; inside, the lovely, circular stairway was removed, and replaced by a broad, oaken one. The Adams mantles with their dainty, exquisite carving were taken out and brick ones installed.

The Admiral had spent some years in Japan and during that time Mrs. Beardsley had received the distinction of being the first American woman presented to the Emperor and Empress of that country.

Before returning to Beaufort following his retirement, Admiral Beardsley had skilled Japanese craftsmen to construct the furniture for his new home. When it arrived, the natives looked in amazement at the ornate and expensive pieces. Nothing like those had ever been placed in the old homes!

To build the elaborate sideboard for the dining room, a Japanese father and son had worked for two years. Each bit of carving on the sideboard—which may be seen at the Anchorage today—has a meaning. In the center is a symbol of a pearl of great price, or flaming jewel, guarded by a female dragon between two male dragons. The circular table, also a part of the present Anchorage's furnishings, is worked with a border of bunches of grapes entwined with vines.

Money was no object and the house was filled with curios—priceless vases, china, jade and paintings.

The Beardsleys sent for Japanese servants; one named Midzutania was Mrs. Beardsley's maid. Another was the gardener. Evidently an expert at growing flowers, he soon had made a showplace of the front and rear. In season roses and bulbs bloomed, and a green house was added, where orchids and other rare flowers were grown.

One tragedy occurred while the Beardsleys occupied the home. In the 1850's, Mrs. Elliott, its occupant, had planted a magnolia tree on each side of the house, naming them "Mary" and "Ann." With the passing of the years they became known as the "Mary Ann" trees.

The magnolias grew to an enormous height and one especially shaded the street. On a dark night, an old man— Mr. Richie—was sandbagged and robbed in the shadow of the tree. The next day, Admiral Beardsley ordered his gardener to cut down the tree.

After the Admiral's death, said to have resulted from drinking too many Cherry Bounces, Mrs. Beardsley lived on at the Anchorage. At her death, there being no living relatives to inherit the property, the house and all its furnishings were put up for auction in Charleston. There, it becoming evident that priceless objets d'art and expensive pieces of furniture were being sold at ridiculously low prices, the auction was stopped. One vase alone, valued at $5,000, brought only $150.

Some of the pieces bought at the auction were returned to the Anchorage and are still in the house.

It is owned by Mrs. Dreka Stokes who operates it as a tourist home, widely known as "The Anchorage."

The Gold Eagle

THE DeSaussures were among the early settlers of Beaufort. Dr. J. A. Johnson's letters in the Beaufort library mention the family as merchants in 1784.

Henry William DeSaussure, (whose father, Daniel, bought the property on which the Gold Eagle Tavern stands from Michael Brewton), served in the Revolution. He was taken prisoner but later exchanged and sent to Philadelphia. There he met George Washington and they became friends.

Washington was so impressed with DeSaussure that he appointed him director of the United States Mint. Shortly afterward, when an order was issued for gold to be coined in the mint, Mr. DeSaussure was put in charge. Six weeks later he personally and proudly delivered a handful of the first gold eagles to his president.

Mr. DeSaussure moved to Columbia in 1798 and became one of the Chancellors of the state. The University of South Carolina has a building named "DeSaussure" in his honor.

The Gold Eagle Tavern is on the site of the Old DeSaussure home. For many years it was noted for its excellent food and service. Residents of Beaufort and nearby plantation owners brought their guests there to dine on the Tavern's famous "Chicken Curry and Flaky Rice."

Soon after the Tavern opened, Henry DeSaussure's grandson, who was born in the old DeSaussure home, came with a group of Northern sportsmen to spend a few days at the Gold Eagle. While there, the old gentleman expressed to some friends a desire to see some of the scenes of his youth—especially did he want to visit the place where the Battle of Honey Hill was fought. The northerners decided to rest at the tavern but Mr. DeSaussure and four old friends set out.

That afternoon as he stood on the battlefield, he showed them how the Rebels stood behind mounds and, as the Yankees came up the road and turned left to cross the bridge, the Rebels mowed them down. Still they came, until finally the creek ran red with blood.

The Rebels' ammunition gave out and they started shooting chains, bolts and nails out of guns. The battle continued until dark and the Yankees retreated to Hilton Head.

One thing Mr. DeSaussure did not mention to his friends was that the soldiers were ordered to fire the broom sedge. Since the wind was blowing in the direction of the Yankee forces, the flames halted them long enough for the Rebels to gather together their makeshift ammunition.

Mr. M. (one of his friends) said that on the return trip to Beaufort old Mr. DeSaussure sat quietly, evidently deep in thought. Finally DeSaussure revealed that he had decided that when he returned to the Tavern he was not going to mention "war" to the northern gentlemen.

However, that night after dinner, the group walked across the grass to the river. The moon had risen and was shimmering on the rippling water. The soft southern breeze brought the fragrance of roses from nearby gardens; and from the Gold Eagle came the sound of music. So perfect was the scene that it was almost unreal.

One Northerner remarked that he had visited many places, North and South, but that he had never seen the moon so pretty. Quick as a flash, without thinking, Mr. DeSaussure said, "Ah! but you should have seen the moon before the war!"

The gentlemen stood a few minutes longer, then went toward the Tavern. Before entering, they stopped. Turning, they saw that Mr. DeSaussure, who was not with them, had not moved from where they had been standing, and seemed to be gazing at the water. Suddenly he raised his hand in a quick salute; then turned and walked toward the rest of the party.

Perhaps he was saying "goodbye" to the place and people whom he loved; we do not know. It was his last visit home.

Sams-Crofut-Herendeen House

BERNERS B. SAMS built this spacious brick home in the late 1840's. The massive, Doric columns are reminiscent of the era that has passed.

The slave quarters for the house servants, in the rear of the home, are one of the most picturesque spots in Beaufort. Built of tabby, they form a high wall for the courtyard. In front of the house is a large park.

Many stories are told of masked balls in the old house, in which the revelers' costumes were elegant and costly. For weeks the costumes would have been in preparation. Sometimes a wearer would recently have returned from abroad and then would perhaps appear in a court costume that had been admired by royalty.

The gentlemen took little part in masquerading. Usually they wore dominoes and masks.

The hall—very wide and airy—was used for promenades, until twelve o'clock when a signal was given for unmasking and supper. Afterwards, music was furnished by a Negro band from Datha plantation. Dancing would continue until the early morning hours.

Many of the Beaufort houses had large ballrooms, for dancing was a favorite form of entertainment for young and old.

* * * *

Slave quarters make an ideal setting for tales of ghosts, and those back of the Crofut House have their share. The following was told me by an old-timer and it is written in her words:

"It was in 1922, and we had rented a bungalow on 'The Point' from Mrs. F. who owned a large house at the edge of the river (the Hext-Morris House, back of the Crofut House) which her family had occupied until the death of her husband. Her children married and moved away, so she rented the house to Mr. and Mrs. A.

"The bungalow she rented us was on the point of her land nearest the river. No one mentioned to me anything unusual ever having happened. But after I told them what I saw, they told me plenty that had happened to them.

"It was just about twilight. Ann, my daughter, was in her room studying. Billy, Jr., was playing in the backyard. I was sitting by the window looking out, waiting for my husband to come in.

"There was a two-pipe fence which ran through a lovely old oak tree at the lawn's edge. All of a sudden I saw this woman. She was very light-skinned, walking straight and looking ahead at the river. She walked behind the tree toward the slave quarters. I watched to see her pass but she never did. I got cold as ice because I realized then that she wasn't dressed like anyone I had ever seen, but like my grandmother possibly dressed in her youth . . . full, white shirtwaist, real full skirt which kicked out when she walked, and a stiff, black, sailor hat. I never saw her again although I used to sit on the porch to see if I would.

"The next day I went over to tell Mrs. A. what I'd seen; and she said 'Now that you've told me I want to tell you what happened to us.'

"Then the lady told of her and her husband seeing an old Negro man standing at the back steps and when Mr. A. asked 'What are you doing here?' thinking that he had come in a boat and was after the wood stacked there, the Negro turned and ran around the front of the house, Mr. A. after him. The man jumped over the fence and vanished right where the old slave quarters are. They realized then that the old man could not have run that fast anyway.

"Of course I couldn't wait to tell Mrs. F. about it. She wasn't at all surprised, and asked if I had heard the soldiers drilling on the green in front of the Crofut House.

"I told her 'no' and 'I hoped I never would.' She said that was where they used to drill and could be heard at certain times.

"Years afterwards, I was visiting my mother in Beaufort. Bert Rodgers, my brother Ed, my mother, sister and I were sitting around talking. I don't know how we got started but each one had a weird story to tell. Ed's was about the voice that says 'That's a dead deer.' I told mine and Bert Rodgers said, 'Loulie, that woman you saw was murdered right in that spot. Where or how, you will have to find out from Bert'!" * * * *

The Berners B. Samses lived in the house until soldiers overran Beaufort; and the home was sold during the war for taxes. After passing through the hands of several other persons, it was bought by Mr. George A. Crofut in 1896.

His descendants have lived in it for several generations, and it has become known as the Crofut-Waterhouse home. It is owned by Mr. and Mrs. E. G. Herendeen.

The Talbirds

FEW stories connected with Beaufort's early families match the drama of Henry Talbird's. It comes authentically from a family record. Though there are other versions, basically all are the same.

A heavy fog was settling over London, blurring the glow of the street lights. Captain Haylton was in a hurry and had he not been familiar with the locality would have been hopelessly lost in the thick mist. A drizzling rain began to fall and this added to his difficulty "Wise men stay indoors at a time like this," he murmured to himself. The captain was the owner of a merchant ship scheduled to sail from Plymouth next day and it was imperative that he return home that night.

Suddenly he heard a cry in the darkness. For a second Captain Haylton thought that he had been mistaken; then it came again, and again.

Had the Captain been a superstitious person, he probably would have hied himself away from the spot as fast as his seafaring legs would carry him. But being practical and of an inquiring mind, he stopped and groped his way around in the darkness toward the sound. Stumbling over an object lying at the foot of a lamp post, he reached down and lifted a small rain-soaked bundle in his arms. As he did, a pitiful little voice whispered "I want to go home." Realizing that he held a small child, the Captain said gently, "Now, now, this will never do. Tell me what it's all about and I will take you home. But first, what's your name?"

The child, a little boy of probably three years of age,

clung tightly to the man. Soon his tears were dried, and as if gaining confidence from the man's words and kindly tone, answered, "My name is Henry Talbot. Please, Sir, take me home."

"Where do you live?"

The lad began to cry again, "I don't know. I can't find my uncle's house." Sobs shook his small body.

Captain Haylton pondered the dilemma. Since he could not leave the child stranded on the street in the London fog, he carried him to the boat waiting to take him to his home in Plymouth. On board, the exhausted boy soon fell asleep.

When the little fellow was taken into the Haylton home, its mistress welcomed him with open arms. She asked no questions and without awakening her little visitor removed his wet garments and placed him in bed.

Then, afterwards, while she listened to her husband's story, the woman—who was childless—washed and hung out by the huge, red hot stove, Henry's clothes. Before she lay down to sleep that night, she had neatly ironed the garments, folded them and placed them by the child's bed, ready for him when he awakened.

She and the Captain talked far into the night. She pleaded to be allowed to keep the child, but he insisted that every effort must be made to locate the boy's parents; and restore him to them. Mrs. Haylton promised that if she saw an advertisement in the London paper seeking information on a lost child she would immediately answer it.

Captain Haylton sailed for America well content that his wife would find the boy's family.

But as the days went by, Mrs. Haylton carefully avoided the newspapers. The little boy was happy in her love and soon forgot his early life. When Captain Haylton returned after a four-months' absence, she truthfully told him that she had heard nothing of the child's relatives. So he agreed to keep him and little Henry became known as the Hayltons' grandson.

A few years later, they decided to go to America and selected South Carolina as their future home. The family settled first in Charleston, then Port Royal.

The boy cared little for the sea but, even so, often accompanied his "grandfather" on voyages. As Mrs. Haylton grew older, she dreaded the loneliness and anxiety their absences from home caused her. She, therefore, persuaded the Captain to sell his ship and give up his life on the sea.

Captain Haylton then established a mercantile business in Charleston. Henry assisted him and soon was familiar with every angle of it. They prospered and after the Captain's death, Henry found himself the owner of a flourishing business.

Soon after the old Captain's death, Henry returned home one evening to find his foster grandmother weeping bitterly. Much concerned—for he loved the old lady dearly—he asked, "Why are you crying? Are you ill?"

"No, no," she answered, "but I have done you a terrible injustice. Will you forgive me?"

"Nonsense," the young man replied, "No one could have done more for her own child! There is nothing to forgive."

"You do not understand," she said sadly, and handing him a London paper, pointed to a one-half column advertisement for a long-lost person named "Henry Talbot."

Henry glanced quickly over the words, "Anyone knowing the whereabouts of such a person is asked to get in touch with the _____ law firm in Dublin, Ireland, and receive a reward."

The announcement further stated that if Talbot were still living and could establish his identity he would become a Knight Baronet and the heir to a large fortune; but, if after diligent search, the person in question was not located, a stepbrother would inherit.

Between broken sobs, Mrs. Haylton revealed the whole

story, and as he sat stunned and unbelieving by her side, she urged him to sail for Dublin to claim his heritage. At first Henry refused to leave the elderly woman because of her health. But when he realized how unhappy she was over the past, he consented. On arriving in Dublin, he was overjoyed to find that he had a living sister, Jane, who lovingly accepted him as her long-lost brother. She filled in details of his life. He was born in Ireland, son of a Knight Baronet whose name was John Talbot. Their father was twice married, the second marriage being contracted to avoid financial embarrassment.

Soon after this second marriage, the family had moved to Dublin, were shortly afterwards, John Talbot was elected Lord Mayor. Meanwhile, John Talbot's brother, Henry, for whom his son Henry was named, had gone to London and acquired a large fortune. Henry Talbot requested his brother to send his young namesake to him, saying that he would make the boy his heir. The uncle was devoted to the child but his wife became violently jealous of the little boy, and sent him out frequently from her sight under the protection of a manservant. On one of these outings, the two visited an unfamiliar part of the city, and the child became lost. The servant claimed that the child ran away in the fog, but it was generally believed that his aunt had bribed the man to lose the boy intentionally.

When Henry presented himself to the guardian of his stepbrother, he was charged with being an imposter and warned under threat of imprisonment to leave Dublin. Henry consulted the Duke of Ormond—a relative of his mother—who in 1677 was Lord Lieutenant of Ireland. The Duke discouraged the chance of recovery of the estate, saying, "There is all the evidence necessary to moral conviction, but there is no legal proof of your identity."

Henry then turned toward his home in America. Upon arriving in Charleston, he found that his foster grandmother had died. Picking up the threads of his life again, he went to Port Royal where he became engaged in business, prospering as before.

About this time Henry was informed of his sister Jane's impending death. He returned to England and learned that she had made him her heir. While there he was informed that the Home Government, in cooperation with the governors of South Carolina and Georgia, was planning to erect lighthouses on the coast. Henry was successful in obtaining a contract for some of these, but in drawing up the legal papers, the name "Talbot" was misspelled and his name was written as "Talbird." Henry, still disgusted with the treatment he had received from his half-brother in England, decided to adopt the new spelling. (However, there is a record of Henry's children having been baptised with the original name in the old register of St. Helena.)

In part payment for his work of building the lighthouses, Henry was given grants of land, one of which was a plantation on Hilton Head. One of his lighthouses is still standing at Tybee, Georgia, which has been referred to as "Talbot Light."

Mrs. Christine Talbird Jenkins owns a watch which formerly belonged to the family of the Duke of Ormand.

Among a Beaufort woman's family papers is a manuscript telling of Henry's son, John.

Lieutenant John Talbird lived on Hilton Head during the Revolution. He was captured by the British during the siege of Charleston and carried off to a prison ship, anchored in Charleston Harbor. Mrs. Talbird was at their home on Hilton Head Island, busy with affairs of the plantation and preparing for the birth of their baby. No word of her husband's capture reached her.

Little Henry Talbird, named for his grandfather, was born on October 19, 1781. Only one thing marred the mother's happiness—her dear John was not there to see his little son. Days passed with no word from her husband.

Early one morning she was roused from a fitful sleep by

terrified servants. Soldiers were coming up the avenue! She recognized their uniforms as that of the Tories.

Lifting her newborn baby from his cradle, she handed the little one to her old nurse. "Hurry," she gasped, "take care of him." Quickly the Negress disappeared through the rear of the house toward the dense woods.

Mrs. Talbird had scarcely reached the front door when she was met by a British officer. Behind him stood soldiers with lighted torches.

"Madam," he began, then stopped in embarrassment, as he was speaking to his own wife's sister. His orders were to burn all Patriots' houses between Savannah and Beaufort. He was a soldier—and sworn to obey orders, but nothing had been said about destroying furniture, so he ordered the slaves to stack the household goods of his sister-in-law under a tree away from the house.

Many of the Talbirds' slaves were captured by the soldiers but nothing was said about searching the surroundings.

When this was done he gave a crisp command, a dozen torches were applied and the house was soon in flames. Without a backward look, he marched toward his ship.

No sooner had the ship set sail than the slaves who had reached the woods came out one by one. Among them was the nurse, carefully holding a very hungry little baby. The Negroes immediately set to work to build a shelter for their mistress, covering it with the leaves of the Palmetto cabbage.

A few days later there was a joyful reunion! John Talbird came home. When told the date of the boy's birth, he exclaimed "Why that is the day that Cornwallis surrendered!"

In 1820 Thomas Talbird built a large mansion of tabby in Beaufort, the ruins of which may be seen today. Back of the house was a tabby recreation center for the servants, known as "Mount Pleasant." "Mount Pleasant" was destroyed, its tabby foundation remaining, however, for many years. The main house was burned in 1907.

The Hepworth-Pringle House has figured in much of the history of the Beaufort region since its construction prior to the Revolutionary War. Piercings for muskets are evident in its tabby basement walls from the time it was used in defense against the uprising Yemmassee Indians. It is now owned by Mr. and Mrs. Somers B. Pringle.

(69)

Retreat Plantation House

The Gold Eagle Tavern, now closed

U. S. Naval Hospital, Port Royal, S. C.

Marine Air Station

The William Elliott House, also known as the "Club House", once was an adjunct to the old Sea Island Hotel. An old diary, compiled during Reconstruction, speaks of a fiery speech made from its balcony by General Wade Hampton during the Red Shirt campaign. It was Hospital No. 11 during the War.

Elizabeth Barnwell Gough, granddaughter of "Tuscarora" Barnwell, built this house, considered one of the town's finest. Elizabeth, a beauty and a belle of Beaufort, met her future husband Richard Gough while sailing to Europe. Upon arriving in London, they were married; later returning to the United States. Their child Marianna married James Smith. This house, now owned by Mr. J. F. Morrall, bears a strong resemblance to Tabby Manse.

The Anchorage, operated as a tourist home by Mrs. Dreka Stokes, dominates the Bay in Beaufort. It is unique for its orientally influenced brick fireplaces, frieze of knights in armor on the ceiling and an organ on every floor. It is filled with rare antiques, some of which were owned by Admiral Beardsley when this residence was his and his wife's retirement home. He gave the house its name "Anchorage" and remodeled it at a cost of $80,000. The expensive oriental furnishings placed in it were made by Japanese workmen. After his and Mrs. Beardsley's deaths, contents of their home were auctioned in Charleston. Because priceless items were selling for ridiculously low prices, the sale was stopped. One such was a vase costing $500 which sold for only $150. The Anchorage is believed to be of pre-Revolutionary origin. It was built by William Elliott.

During the Federal occupancy, this home was the Officers' Building and also served as Hospital No. 14. It is the Sanders' home shown on opposite page. On right of hospital is the Verdier House where William DeSaussure was born and which was owned by the Director of the Mint.

This home with its ornate columns, banisters, fencing and other decorative woodwork, was built by Lewis Sams in 1852. It is the home of Mr. and Mrs. Lawrence Sanders.

The only seamless house known in the South Carolina Sea Islands built entirely of tabby is located on Datha Island. It is thought that this was used as a smoke house by the Sams family, owners of Datha. The architectural curiosity is constructed without any seams or cracks of any kind and is a rare example of a tabby roof. Datha Island is now owned by Mrs. Richard Rowland.

Ruins of Datha Island are among the best exposition of tabby in the Sea Islands. The plantation home of the Sams family, burned while occupied by Negroes after the Confederate War, consisted of three distinct houses in one: "East" and "West" which were added to the original "Middle." Each house had its own piazza and large Sycamore tree. The garden stretched from the front to a pond beyond. Huge orchards grew olives, oranges, pears, figs and other fruit. The Reverend James Julius Sams, D.D., who spent his youth there, describing the plantation, said to the Sams family "it was a sort of terrestrial paradise." The Chapel was placed to form a part of the wall which enclosed the family burying ground.

The Sams House on Datha,
burned during Reconstruc-
tion. The Sams family bought
Datha Island shortly after the
Revolutionary War.

Interior of Datha Chapel.

Burial ground of the Sams
family on Datha Island. The
illustrations on this page are
from paintings by the late
Miss Eugenia Sams who died
in 1920. Miss Sams willed
paintings to her nephew
Horace Reeve Sams, who gave
them to Mrs. Toland Sams.

Tidewater, the home of Senator and Mrs. Brantley Harvey, has two entrances, both equally beautiful. The house was built by William Fripp in the late 1830's from parts of other plantation homes on St. Helena Island, this accounting for the difference in style of the north and south doors and different type cornices in each room. All of the interior doors and mantels are cypress and lean toward Greek Revival design—making it a "transition" house.

Hext-Morris House, also important historically, is stocked with fine antiques. It is partially occupied by an antique shop operated by its owner, Mrs. Irma Morris. Legend says gold is buried in its yard, placed there by pirates.

This ante-bellum frame house, the Smith-Fordham home, is unique in that it has no front gate or entrance from the main street. The front facade is a two-story porch with large, round columns, windows flanked by side-lights and square-capped chimneys. It was once occupied by the special agent for the United States Treasury and also served as a hospital during the Confederate War. John Joyner Smith built this home in 1813, and it is now occupied by Mr. and Mrs. Angus Fordham of Beaufort. During the War the Military Commander General Stevens resided here, when it was known as the Smith House.

Called the Doctor White House, this old home is antebellum. Exact date of construction is not known, however one source offers this information, "This was an original grant to the Thompson family and they lived there for a long while then sold the place to their cousins the Whites." Changes and additions have been made to the structure through the years. Last owners were the Reids.

A branch of the Beaufort Library. The building was originally a Negro Presbyterian Church.

The W. A. Black House on the Bay was once the home of Major William H. Trescott, under Secretary of State in President Buchanan's administration. Built by his slaves and head carpenter, the house was later purchased in 1876 by Congressman William Elliott who floated it from a sea island down the river on barges, re-erecting it in Beaufort. Dr. Black acquired it in the 1930's.

This house, owned by Mrs. Charles Luther, on Bay Street, was formerly the residence of Secretary of the Navy Denby.

The Cherokee Inn was modeled after the famous Secession House, one block up on the same street. It is owned and operated by Mrs. Louis Mabry of Beaufort.

Called Bellamy Inn by the present generation of Beaufortonians, this house was built by the Milne family at least one hundred years ago. It served as a farm house at one time and now is located on Boundary Street, one of the main thoroughfares, on the curve where that street joins Carteret. It is currently owned by the W. M. Davidsons.

ANTE-BELLUM HOME IN BEAUFORT · STATE OF SOUTH CAROLINA

TRAVEL A NEW WORLD
SEE THE U.S.A.

The travel poster, above, showing the Johnson-Danner House in Beaufort, is being published all over the world by the U. S. Department of Commerce in its "Visit U. S. A." program, established by the International Travel Act of 1961. The house, known as "The Castle," is the South Carolina selection to accompany points of interest of the other 49 states in the department's bid to encourage both foreign and domestic tourist trade.

(84)

The Castle

PICTURESQUE and lovely, the Johnson-Danner house sits in magnificent splendor, framed by tall palmettoes and ancient trees.

Like a medieval castle it rises high above a tidal creek. Its seventy-two windows glisten in the golden sunshine or stare bleak and cold when the north wind sweeps across the Bay to The Point.

The soft color of the house blends in with its surroundings, seeming to vary with weather conditions—so that sometimes it appears to be a very pale pink, then again the color appears to shade from creamy beige to yellow.

Four long French windows are on each side of the front entrance door. Six huge columns reach to the ceiling, and balustrades enclose both the upper and lower porches.

The house, often called "The Castle," was built by Dr. Joseph Johnson about the middle of the nineteenth century. It is said that the fine marble mantelpieces ordered from abroad had not arrived when Beaufort was invaded by Union forces.

Today, as in the past, the Castle's gardens are a joy to see. Springtime finds them a riot of color—camellias, azaleas and roses bloom in breathtaking beauty. All the wealth of plants native to the lowcountry grow here in abundance.

The gardens are very old, being first planted by Dr. Johnson. Even during the war years they were not completely destroyed. Perhaps the fact that the house was a hospital during that time saved them.

Like many other old houses, the Castle has its ghost. Since Dr. Johnson's time, the tale of the little dwarf—who is supposed to have come to these shores with Jean Ribaut—has been handed down by succeeding generations.

It is told that Dr. Johnson, supervising the planting of his garden, saw the dwarf go around the house. Turning to the old colored man spading the ground, he asked, "Who is that?"

"You mean dat little man come out de crick?"

Though the Negro had not looked up, he immediately knew to whom Dr. Johnson was referring.

"Dat, Sir, is de one who live in de basement."

Dr. Johnson was not alone in seeing the dwarf. Visitors tell of standing on the edge of the tidal creek which flows beside the house, and feeling a gust of icy wind, and then seeing a thin streak of mist rise from the water. It floats toward the house, and, as it reaches land, takes the shadowy and indistinct form of a man, then disappears into the darkness.

Members of the family admit to unusual happenings within the house. Furniture is mysteriously moved and doors are opened and closed by unseen hands.

Not so many years ago a visitor related the story of a night spent in the house. He had heard of the little dwarf and laughed with the family about it. Before they bade him goodnight, his hostess inquired was he nervous, and he assured her that he was not—that he did not believe in ghosts.

He did not know how long he had been asleep when he was awakened by a loud clap of thunder. The wind was blowing in gusts and there were frequent flashes of vivid lightning. He judged the storm lasted about thirty minutes. Then there came that deadly stillness which often is the aftermath of an electrical storm on the coast. Nothing stirred in the quiet house.

He could not remember drifting off to sleep but something caused him to sit upright in bed. Then distinctly the sound of footsteps in the hallway reached him. As they came nearer he held his breath, and the door opened softly, letting in a current of cold air. Despite himself, he felt a tingling up his spine as if an icy hand had touched his back. Puzzled and a little frightened, the man called, "Who is there?"

For a second there was no answer; then so low that it seemed almost the murmur of the wind, he heard "This is Gauche."

"What are you doing here?"

"I live here—in the cellar."

"Why?"

"It reminds me of my English home that I will never enter again."

"Will you let me see you?"

"No, I do not show myself to fools," came the reply.

Then the door closed.

Incredulous ones say that the visitor, expecting something to happen because he had often heard the story of "the little old man who lived in the basement," dreamed this experience.

There is nothing ghostly about the interior of the house. The wide hallways and spacious rooms are filled with elegant period furniture, old portraits and heavy silver, telling an unspoken story of the people who have called it home.

The beauty of "The Castle" has gone afar. The United States Travel Service of the Department of Commerce selected it for its poster from South Carolina to be used with other points of interest from the different states, and sent a photographer there this spring. These were placed in "leading newspapers and magazines in England, France, Germany, Mexico, Japan and Australia."

This was done under the following international Travel Act of 1961:

SELLING THE UNITED STATES

"The Secretary shall develop, plan and carry out a comprehensive program designed to stimulate and encourage travel to the United States by residents of foreign countries for the purpose of study, culture, recreation, business and other activities as a means of promoting friendly understanding and goodwill among people of foreign countries and of the United States."

The beautiful home, owned by Mr. and Mrs. Howard Danner, is one of the few homes in Beaufort occupied continuously—except for the Yankee Interlude—by descendants of the builder.

Secession House

FOR nearly two centuries Secession House has stood, stately and lovely, facing the Beaufort River. The basement and first story may well have been built before the Revolutionary War, since the lots on which it stands were bought by Robert Williams in 1743.

The house was later owned by Milton Maxcy who sold it to Edmund Rhett a decade or so before the Confederate War. Rhett and two of his brothers had gone through court proceedings to change their name—originally Smith—to that of a famous Rhett ancestor.

Due to the influence of one brother, Robert Barnwell Rhett, the place is called "Secession House." In this home, Barnwell Rhett, U. S. Senator from South Carolina, most strongly advocated secession. Many fiery meetings were held and Rhett became known as the "Father of Secession." From the last of these meetings, the delegates to Charleston Convention went directly to the boat landing. Amid the cheers of all who were not accompanying them, they set off for Charleston to help the Convention vote that South Carolina would secede and become an independent state.

It was a great disappointment to Barnwell Rhett that he was not elected President of the Confederacy. With the assistance of *The Charleston Mercury*, he waged a bitter, relentless, political campaign against Jefferson Davis throughout the war.

When Beaufort was invaded, Federal soldiers occupied Secession House; and later the United States Tax Commission took possession of it.

This house was used by General Rufus Saxon as his headquarters during the occupation of Beaufort by Federal troops.

The soldiers left evidence of their occupancy in the old home: handwriting on the walls and bayoneted mutilation of the ceiling ornamentation. It is a fact that Secession House was photographed and sketched by Union soldiers more than any other house in Beaufort.

After the war, Edmund Rhett's widow paid the direct taxes and thus reclaimed her home. When she died, a Barnwell family bought it. The father of Mrs. Thomas Heyward (Emma Barnwell) was born at Secession House.

The house today is even lovelier than it was in the past. The building is of Greek Revival architecture and its curved, marble steps, leading to the piazza, are so graceful and picturesque that it is not unusual to see artists sketching them. The Italian, marble mantels were not damaged during the war; and the elaborately patterned frieze on the ceilings has been carefully and perfectly restored. The large, high-ceilinged rooms are furnished much as they were when the Rhetts gave their magnificent dinners and balls.

When the old homes in Beaufort are put on tour in March of each year—sponsored by the Women of St. Helena Episcopal Church—much interest is always shown in the antebellum cook house in the backyard of Secession House, where meals were prepared, then protected and kept warm with silver covers while being carried to the big house.

Secession House is now owned by Mr. and Mrs. Claude E. McLeod.

Barrier Islands

ST. HELENA ISLAND

ACROSS the river from Beaufort lies St. Helena Island, one of the largest South Carolina Sea Islands.

In 1525, Pedro de Quexos, a young Spanish pilot attached to d'Ayllon's two caravels, sailed northward from Florida, and one day entered what is now known as St. Helena Sound. He saw a large, beautifully wooded cape protruding into the water; and in the *Name of Spain* christened it "Punta de Santa Elena" to honor Saint Elena.

One hundred and thirty-eight years later, a young English sea captain, Sir William Hilton, told in his "Journal" of anchoring his ship in St. Elena Sound and that the island was occupied by Indians. He wrote of a house built in the shape of a "Dove House, completely covered with Palmetto leaves, the wall part being twelve feet high, and within were lodging rooms, and forms. Two pillars were at the entrance of a high seat above all the rest."

Hilton mentions another house standing on ten-foot posts and fastened to them with spikes . . . this he thought was a "Sentinel House."

Less than a hundred and seventy-five years later, the island was a network of cotton plantations. The Fripps owned more land, and were the largest planters on St. Helena. One plantation bought in 1856 comprised fourteen hundred acres. John Fripp, Sr., and his wife Sara, came to St. Helena with a grant from the King. Some of the Fripps' plantations were known as "Mulberry Hill," "Capt. John Fripp's," "Captain Oliver Fripp's," "Pine Grove," "Homestead," "Hope Place," and "Orange Grove."

T. A. Coffin, owner of "Coffin's Point," and "Cherry Hill," and the Popes whose home was "The Oaks," were said to have the best-managed plantations on the island. They received the top-market price each year for their cotton.

"Coffin's Point," "The Oaks" and "Land's End" (the Jenkins' plantation), contained large libraries of rare and expensive books. Mr. Jenkins' books were carried to Hilton Head during the war but afterwards he was able to recover a large number of the volumes.

"Coffin's Point" was occupied during most of the Confederate War years by the men and women sent from the North to teach the Negroes. Miss Laura Towne tells of living there, of going up into the attic and rummaging through the Coffin private papers. Years ago, The South Carolina Historical Society received a number of Coffin family papers that had been carried north by one of the teachers.

Many of Miss Towne's letters speak of the beauty of the islands. Some relate stories of picnics and dinners held in the old plantation homes. One mentions St. Helenville, a small summer resort of planters on the island, describing it as a "deserted village of a dozen or more mansions with their house servants' cabins behind them, and two churches in a large pine woods. The village is directly on the creek on a high bluff like that on which Beaufort is situated, about eight feet high. It is the place where the white people used to spend the summer for health and society."

Evidently one of the teachers was a mulatto, because another wrote of her: "Miss Fortner has one of the sweetest voices I ever heard. She is partly Negro blood. The Negroes all knew the instant they saw her what she was, but she has been treated by them with universal respect."

After the Confederate War some of the teachers remained on St. Helena and bought land at tax sales. Mr. Chaplin, who had planted before the 1860's on the island, wrote in his journal in 1886 that "Coffin's Point is owned by a Yankee, S. W. Whitnell." It had changed ownership several times before he took possession.

In recent times, Mr. and Mrs. J. E. McTeer, of Beaufort, bought the plantation. Soon afterward, Mr. McTeer was informed that no water was to be found on the place. However, in irrigating a field he discovered underground springs which in three weeks poured forth a million gallons of water!

"Coffin Point," and the old Fripp plantation on the other side of the island, now owned by Dr. and Mrs. Marshall Sanford, probably look much as they did one hundred years ago.

"Frogmore Manor," the home of Mr. and Mrs. Edward G. Sanders, has been beautifully restored. Mrs. Sanders was born in this house. A large, tabby foundation indicates there must have been a substantial building there in the early eighteenth century.

The Popes were an important family of St. Helena Island.

The Pope house on St. Helena Island was called "Feliciana." John Jeremiah Theus Pope built it for his wife, Mary Frampton Townsend. When she became ill, he constructed "The Oaks" because it was nearer to Beaufort physicians. The story of their love has come down through the years. "My Mary," he always called her, just as if it were one word.

She especially admired crape myrtle trees and planted many around her home. When she died, Mr. Pope moved a large one from her garden and planted it at her grave. He wrote during the war to a member of the family that he hoped the tree would not die while he was in exile with no one to water it—but it evidently did, for "no crape myrtle grows beside her grave in the old Baptist Churchyard on St. Helena."

When a relative on Edisto Island, who had been married several times, suggested his taking another wife, Mr. Pope replied, "No, Isaac, I had 'My Mary,' and I can never love another."

The Popes sold their cotton to Germany. No cotton factor was involved; the agent came directly to St. Helena where the transactions were completed.

During the Confederate War, many of their pictures, legal papers and family records, were sent to Columbia, only to be burned when the city was destroyed by Sherman.

Among family members who refugeed on lands near Aiken, owned by Isaac Jenkins Mikell, were Mrs. Susan Amarinthia Pope and her husband, the Reverend Robert W. Fuller of Beaufort. The Reverend Mr. Fuller was a victim of tuberculosis and could not go to war.

When one of the Pope families returned to their home on St. Helena following the war, they found the only furniture left there were pieces so large that they could not be moved.

Years later, when Rosa Abigail Pope King—wife of Hezekiah King—returned to Beaufort with her daughter, Rosa May King, to visit her childhood home, she registered at a local hotel. The clerk, learning they were going out to St. Helena to see the old Pope home, remarked, "Oh, a man stayed here some years ago who was hunting for Pope descendants of St. Helena. He was from up North and left his address with me for any Popes I might see—wants to get in touch."

Mrs. King's daughter wrote to the gentleman, and his reply stated that his brother, who had been stationed on St. Helena during the Confederate War, had taken the door knocker, a wooden spoon and fork combination for removing pickles from a jar, and a picture . . . and he wished to return them. Subsequently, the pickle fork and the door knocker were returned, but he wrote that a relative loved the picture and would not let him send it!

The church that Mary Frampton Townsend Pope and Wiliam Fripp worked on together became a Negro Baptist church and was the Church of the Penn School for Negroes on St. Helena Island following the Confederate War. The church, known now as the "Brick Church," has a beautifully kept graveyard, in which, it is said, are only graves of white people, including that of Mary Frampton Townsend Pope, her daughter, Hepzibah Jenkins Pope and her husband, (who was her cousin) William John Pope, son of Squire William Pope of Hilton Head.

William Fripp and Mary F. Townsend Pope died within a few months of each other in 1861 and are buried in "their" Brick Church's Cemetery on St. Helena.

Sea Island cotton, like the way of life when it was in its glory, is gone; but the land along the rivers and creeks is thickly settled. Many attractive, new homes have been built on the island.

In early summer the island is jammed with migrant workers and every nook and cranny seems to overflow with outsiders who have come to gather the crops. Mainly these are Mexicans, bringing along babes in arms, arriving in buses and all sorts of vehicles. Packing sheds work at full speed and during the night hours their lights pierce the darkness of the island. Huge trucks, parked at their doors, stand ready to convey tomatoes, cucumbers and other important truck crops over long distances; and on the sidings stand refrigerated cars for the same purpose.

HUNTING ISLAND

Two thousand acres of land across the Harbor River (from St. Helena) were owned in the middle of the nineteenth century by a group of Beaufort men, who occupied homes on St. Helena.

John G. Barnwell, Captain John Fripp, General Stephen Elliott, Edward M. Capers and Dr. W. J. Jenkins had purchased the acreage as a hunting preserve. Because it was used purely for hunting, the land became known as "Hunting Island."

I. Jenkins Mikell wrote, "Hunting Island is a paradise for deer hunters and duck shoots."

Camping parties—in those times—would often spend several days on the island, occasionally being accompanied by their wives, but infrequently. In his journal dated 1857, Mr. Chaplin says, "I went hunting with Dr. Jenkins' party. There were Dr. Croft, Captain Fripp, Edgar Fripp, Dr. C. A. Fripp; also the following ladies, Mrs. Croft, Misses Mary Croft, Amanda Jenkins and Eliza Jenkins. Dr. Croft killed one deer."

The planters' fishing and hunting clubs, with the Agricultural Society, afforded a never-ending source of entertainment. Until the beginning of the Confederate War, "hunting was one of the planters' chief amusements."

A part of Hunting Island in recent years was operated by South Carolina as a state park, with housing facilities available for families along the Atlantic ocean-front; a pavilion on the beach; and camp sites equipped with bath houses and electricity.

U. S. Highway 21 bisects Hunting Island, coming from Beaufort via Frogmore. A new road has been cut, joining U. S. 21 and the new bridge over Fripp Inlet to Fripp Island Resort.

HILTON HEAD

"The lands are laden with large tall trees—oaks, walnuts and bayes, except facing the sea it is mostly pines, tall and good. The land generally, except where the pines grow, is a good soil covered with black mold. The country abounds with grapes, large figs and peaches; the woods with deer, conies, turkeys, quail, curlues, plovers, teile, herons, ducks and innumerable other water fowls. Oysters in abundance. . . . The Rivers stored plentifully with fish which we saw play and leap," wrote William Hilton in 1664.

Before Hilton touched this shore the island had been visited earlier by the Spaniards, French Huguenots and Indians. But it was from William Hilton that it received its name.

Hilton Head contains 30,000 acres of land. Its vast stretches became one of the most productive of all the South Carolina islands growing Sea Island cotton. Planters from Beaufort and Edisto bought and operated plantations there, but few owners had permanent homes on the island, accounting for the lack of impressive houses.

The Baynards were an exception, and the large, thick tabby foundation of their old home gives an inkling of their wealth, as does the family mausoleum near its site.

Popes, Draytons, Kirks, Barnwells, Jenkinses, Seabrooks, Stuarts and Talbirds were among the early landowners of Hilton Head but there were many others.

Like its neighbor, Hunting Island, Hilton Head abounds in good fishing, both for sport and food. In William Elliott's book, "Carolina Sports," he describes numerous trips in search of Devilfish, a little-known sport today. In July, 1844, he wrote, "I launched my boat at Bay Point and crossed to Hilton Head shore in search of Devil Fish. I was accompanied by Henry Stuart. It was high water about four o'clock p. m., and on reaching the landing at Mrs. Elliott's, just as the tide was turning, we saw three or more.

"They did not show themselves somersetting for some time, but after awhile, began to sport, and throw somersets under the water, but so near to the surface as to show their bellies in the evolution. We saw, I do not doubt, as many as twenty fish. We counted eleven that leaped entirely out of the water. . . . Usually they leap twice—leaping from their backs and falling likewise on their backs—leaping I should say at least ten feet above the water."

The above expedition was terminated by a storm but Elliott relates other thrilling times of harpooning the huge

Devilfish, a species of the gigantic rays which sometimes grow fifteen to twenty-five feet wide.

*   *   *   *

Zion Chapel of Ease at Hilton Head was built in 1788. Its lovely chalices were stolen during the Confederate War. Years later, a pawnshop owner displayed them in his store window, where an antique buyer, thinking they were silver goblets, purchased them. On removing the dust and tarnish, the words "Zion Chapel of Ease, Hilton Head, S. C., 1834" became visible.

Attempting to return them to the rightful owners, the buyer was told the little chapel had been demolished, so he turned them over to St. Helena Episcopal Church in Beaufort. He requested that should Zion Chapel of Ease ever be rebuilt, the chalices be sent back to Hilton Head. One of the goblets was placed by St. Helena at the Church of the Cross in Bluffton, there to await its need at Hilton Head.

*   *   *   *

Hilton Head has two stories of buried treasure, one of them dating from the time of Ribaut's colony. His men, while exploring the country—the story goes—took from the Indians some $1,600,000 in Spanish gold salvaged from wrecked treasure ships and buried it where they obtained it, presumably somewhere in Beaufort County, and perhaps on Hilton Head. The Spanish Archives relate an expedition was sent out in 1567 to recover this treasure, but the outcome of the search is not known.

The other dates from the second French settlement, under Strozzi. It is said that the French corsairs had raided three Spanish ports, including the pearling centre of Santa Magarita off the Venezuelan coast, before arriving at Hilton Head and that Strozzi offered a substantial ransom to Menendez when he was captured. Menendez refused the ransom, so presumably Strozzi's stolen gold and pearls still lie buried somewhere on the island.

* * * *

Among the more romatic males on Hilton Head in days past was Squire William Pope. He was said to be "gorgeous to look at" and all the ladies swooned over him. That he was very handsome is confirmed by a Beaufort descendant of the family who owns a miniature of Pope.

* * * *

Many superstitions of Negroes on the island have come down through the years. For instance, cotton was to be planted only when the great, sweet-scented lilac-like blossoms of the Tree of India (Chinaberry) were in full bloom.

Or, if a bird flew in a window, it was a sign of death. A hoot owl near the house was a warning of bad luck.

Then there was—and still is among some—the belief in the teachings of their African ancestors of "hants" that come in different forms for good or evil.

* * * *

For many years after peace came to the South, Hilton Head was an isolated island reached only by boat. The Negroes owned much of the land, secured from the plantations divided by the Federal government and sold for taxes.

During this time, private hunting preserves were bought or leased on the island; but it was not until 1950 that the present-day Hilton Head, with its luxurious motels and homes, was visualized by a group of Georgians.

That the vision has become a reality is largely due to a young Yale graduate, Charles Fraser. As president of the Sea Pines Corporation, he has worked untiringly for the island's development.

Another developer, The Hilton Head Company, has also been responsible for improvements to turn the island into a vacation wonderland.

Visitors to Hilton Head will find just about every diversion for a relaxing and interesting stay. Boating, swimming, fishing, golfing and minor sports offer pleasant recreation. A part of the island has been set aside in its natural state as a wildlife refuge; and hunting, fishing are allowed seasonally. On the island, bird watchers find unusual specimens, from the snowy egrets nesting in the swamps to the great eagles in the tall pines.

Historic forts and ruins, Indian mounds and a comfortable sub-tropical climate have helped turn the island into a growing resort.

Hilton Head, located between Savannah and Beaufort, is reached by way of The James F. Byrnes Bridge, named for South Carolina's elder statesman, former assistant president, secretary of state and governor.

LADIES ISLAND

Sixty-four islands, large and small, help protect Beaufort from the blasts of hurricane wind and tides.

Across the Bay from town is Ladies Island where many new, attractive homes have been built in this century. In the long ago, it was a land of cotton plantations. There were houses for the owners' slaves and overseers. But the island was near enough town for the owner to row across the Bay, attend to business and return home in time for dinner.

Two of the most extensive planter-families on Ladies Island before the Confederate War were the Chaplins and the McKees. Both were wealthy and influential. "Chaplin's Court" in Beaufort was a large, pretentious house.

COOSAW

After the Bulls' large mansion on adjacent Coosaw Island was burned in 1715, no residence of any size was erected on the small island. It was used for planting, however, and had large groves of olive and orange trees on it. During the war, the Negroes cut down the trees and burned them for firewood.

Today, except for one very small tract, all of the land on Coosaw is owned by Negroes.

DATHA ISLAND

William Sams and Elizabeth Hext were married February 5, 1761, and both are buried in the family cemetery on Datha Island. Before Mr. Sams bought Datha, the couple lived on Wadmalaw Island, St. John's Parish, until after the Revolution. Purchase of Datha, containing 1200 acres, from his cousins Robert and Sarah (Reeve) Gibbs, was completed May 13, 1783.

Williams Sams' home on Datha was famous for the lustrous painting of morning glories on the walls of the Drawing and Dining Rooms. The flowers formed a pattern, much like the designs on wallpaper today, and were painted on the walls by an artist who lived in the Sams' home for many months.

Lewis Reeve Sams, Dr. Berners Barnwell Sams and Edward Hext Sams, inherited from their father his plantation on Datha. Edward sold his interest to his brothers and they divided the island.

Dr. Sams' son, the Reverend James Julius Sams, D.D., described the Datha House as being three distinct houses. He said, "The roof above was so constructed, and the passage within, as to be to all intents and purposes one house. The house, built of tabby, had three names, 'West,' 'East,' and 'Middle.' The 'Middle' house was the old and original home. It was much older than my grandmother's time. It consisted of two rooms, a narrow passage between, two attic rooms and two cellars below. My father added the two wings, each wing as large as the original house. The two wings were connected by a large passageway running back of the 'Middle' house. The narrow passage in the 'Middle' house opened into this large passage on its side.

"The two ends of this large passage were entered from two doors, respectively, in the parlours. The three houses each had its own piazza. That of the 'Middle' house was the most isolated. In front of each house there was a large Sycamore, beyond there were two large Walnut trees, beyond these again was the old garden which stretched to a little pond, on this side of which, that is between the house and pond, was a large grove of Poplar trees. On a moonlight night they looked like so many ghosts.

"Back of the house was the dairy, on the east side of the dairy, the well with the old oaken bucket. On the other side, directly on the north, was the Pear Orchard. East of it, the Plum Orchard; northwest of the house was the Orange Grove. Southwest, the figs and apples. There were pears, figs and oranges elsewhere. The island was well supplied with fruit.

"West of the orchard was our family burying ground. It was shaded all over by the largest oak I ever saw. This tree grew in the middle of the graveyard and threw its limbs out and around, in all directions, even taking its cover over the wall which encircled the yard. On the east of the Oak was the Chapel, which was so placed as to form part of the wall which ran around the whole spot."

Further, Dr. Sams tells of his youth spent on Datha— on hunting, fishing, swimming, rowing; and activities among the woods and creeks of the island. He wrote that his Uncle Lewis, who owned the other half of the island, had been bothered by the Negroes complaining that whenever the wind blew hard a white lady with long, streaming hair appeared in the "Big Woods," screaming and ringing her hands. He added "It was almost impossible to get a Negro to pass the spot at night."

"At last my uncle told them that the next time they heard the white lady, they must let him know. Accordingly, not long after this, a storm of wind happened to rage and some of the Negroes came and reported that the white lady had commenced to scream. Calling his dogs, and taking a hatchet, my uncle set out in search of the 'White Lady.' It was night. Entering the woods and making his way as well as he could in the dark, he followed the sound until he reached the tree from which it seemed to come. He barked the tree with his hatchet and then turned homeward. He passed out of the field and entered that known as 'Little Woods.' Then he said it was his time to be frightened!

"Suddenly he heard around him great trampling as of many horses. The conduct of the dogs helped to alarm him. They ran in between his legs again and again, almost tripping him up. At last, with yelps they dashed off, never stopping until they reached home! He said it was the first time he ever experienced the sensation of hair standing on end. He never found out from what that sound came, nor could he explain the conduct of the dogs in connection with it.

" 'The White Lady' turned out to be the limbs of a tree which had crossed in contact with each other, and being long, whenever the wind blew, they rubbed together and made a shrill noise."

One of the Sams women told the writer of a conversation she had with one of the old Negroes about ghosts. "Chile," the old woman said, "whenevers you sees a dog sniffing on a moonlight night—dat dog know a hant teasing he."

"How do you get rid of hants, if they worry you?" my friend asked.

"Dat's easy. Only remedy is keep matches in pocket— don't strike 'em—'jest rub 'em t'gether, cause ghosts can't take sulphur."

Lewis Reeves Sams was a very fine horticulturist and took much pleasure in growing fine flowers and plants. He also experimented with grafts and cuttings. There was one camellia bush on which he had grafted every variety and color, causing a sensation in Beaufort.

On the Morgan River side of the island, Lewis Reeve Sams' famous orange groves were located. These trees were said to have been imported from France and planted about 1800, providing the first commercially grown oranges in America. Even after the Confederate War, oranges were still shipped to Charleston from Datha. But due to the war and the other misfortunes resulting from it, no more were raised there and the emphasis shifted to Florida, that state securing its first stock from the orange trees at Datha. A few trees left from the three separate groves of Mr. Sams, which totaled thirty-five acres in all, remained until modern times.

The great storm of 1893 washed the Lewis Reeve Sams' home—remains of which are in water at high tide—into his beloved Morgan River.

Mrs. Sams was the daughter of Thomas Fripp and Martha Hann Fripp. The Fripps were closely linked with the Sams family, with much intermarriage.

Mr. Sams kept peacocks at his home on the Bay; and an old letter tells that at sunset the birds would stand on the wall at the edge of the river, their lovely colors reflected in the water by the setting sun.

The Samses had fine houses in Beaufort, but they loved their island. Dr. Sams wrote, "Datha was to us a kind of terrestrial paradise."

Before leaving St. Helena and Beaufort—when troops arrived at Hilton Head—a small effort was made to hide a few of the family treasures. Some lovely gold, blue and white china was hastily buried in a soft, muddy spot in a road because it was easy to dig into and cover. Over four years later, when the china was dug up, only one piece was broken. Many a horse and carriage must have passed over them!

When the Confederate War was over and the Samses returned to the island, they found the house occupied by Negroes, and thus not available to them.

The Sams' family was a close-knit one, and those reading the different accounts of their lives surely feel the love between them.

On Datha, the smoke house with its unique tabby roof stands complete. The outlines of William's and B. B. Sams' homes may be seen, covered or screened by vines, trees and other plants. One tall wall, with its smooth finish intact, of the latter's house, shows the great height of the windows. The storehouse next to the smoke house is outlined and the well coping and huge kitchen fireplace are standing. Other ruins are outlines of a cotton house at the head of what was the "Cotton House Road" leading down to the Big Landing.

The cemetery wall of tabby is intact and now covered with "Resurrection Fern." The foundation of the Chapel is also visible, its last standing wall being demolished in the vicious hurricane "Gracie" which visited its wrath on Datha in the 1950's.

A corner in the private burying ground was reserved for pets of the family.

One gravestone in this cemetery stands out. It says with old lettering:

> Sacred to the Memory of Sarah Sams
> A Member of the Baptist Church
> The wife of Lewis Reeve Sams
> And mother of Lewis Reeve, Miles Brewton, Anglrona Hext, Caroline Edings, Robert Barnwell, Stanhope Augustus, Marion Washington, and Sarah Emily Sams.
> Who was born December 26 A. D. 1789
> And died August 12th A. D. 1825
> Aged 35 years, 7 months, 17 days
> "Blessed Are The Dead Who Die In The Lord"

* * *

POLAWANA

At a Sams' house on the little island of Polawana, a man in the family awoke late one night to see a mighty flame rising up from Datha Island. He touched the child who lay beside him and cried, "Wake up, son, Datha is burning—Thank God!"

FRIPP ISLAND

It is possible that there are more legends connected with this lovely little island than any other on the South Carolina coast. There is little mention of it by historians; but situated as it is, there is no doubt that it played a colorful part in the development of the area.

The island has numerous Indian mounds, and various relics of the Red man's occupancy have been uncovered.

Many vague tales have come down through the years—tales crowded with romance and adventure. Fripp is said to have been the favorite hideaway of that swaggering, reckless pirate of the early eighteenth century, Blackbeard, who roamed the Colonial coast—especially along Delaware, Virginia, and the Carolinas. Around Fripp were many ideal places to evade capture. Small, winding creeks, inlets and rivers abound nearby. A high bluff made a perfect look-out.

Blackbeard was born in Bristol, England, but one seldom hears him referred to by his real name of Edward Teach. His nickname was due to the extraordinary quantity of jet black hair with which his head and face were covered. He was in the habit of twisting it with ribbons into small tails and turning them up about his ears.

Somewhere beneath the sand dunes on Fripp, Blackbeard is thought to have buried many treasure chests.

In 1708, he anchored off the Port of Charleston and there he plundered incoming and outgoing ships, taking as prisoners some of the important persons of town.

It was not a pleasant sight for the citizens of Charles Town to see the pirate captain's ship guarding their port, its black flag with its cross and white skull fluttering in the breeze. So, when Blackbeard sent a messenger bearing a white flag into the settlement saying that he would liberate his prisoners and vacate the port in exchange for much needed medicine for his crew, the offer was quickly accepted. Early one morning in May, Blackbeard, wearing his usual "three brace of pistols hanging in holsters" marched at the head of his men through Charles Town's streets, to obtain the supplies.

In the dignified old city, a tale is whispered that the high-born, adventurous Miss O—, living in a large gray house near St. Michael's Church, waved gaily at the bold young pirate, who returned her greeting with a bow and a wide sweep of his hat.

He exchanged the prisoners for his medicine as promised, and on his way back to the ship, stopped for a moment where Miss O— was standing in her gateway. Without a word, Blackbeard swooped her up and carried the frantic, struggling girl aboard the vessel. Immediately he set sail for North Carolina where his friend, Governor Charles Eden, married him to Miss O— despite her pleadings. Then sailing to what is now called Fripp Island—where so much of his treasure had been buried—Blackbeard left his wife there heavily guarded while he resumed his piracy of the high seas.

The writer has heard several versions of this legend. One is that Edward Teach's bride in time ceased to exhibit the coldness she first showed him, became a loving wife and one day, bedecked in diamonds, pearls and rubies, she sailed away with him to the West Indies.

* * * *

Some claim that Count Pulaski, who served as Brigadier General in the Revolutionary War on the American side, was buried on Fripp Island. While officially it has never been determined where the Count was buried, many clues point to the possibility that his last resting place might be this island. Recently the remains of an ancient skeleton were unearthed near the high bluff on Fripp Island and preliminary reports have led to speculation that Pulaski's grave may have been found at last.

In 1856 when John Fripp, Jr., was owner of the island and planted the famous Sea Island cotton on its fertile ground, it was known as "Fripps." No records seem to exist of any houses ever having been on the island, save one, "Old House." This small, simple structure was said to have been a summer place for one of the Fripp family; and for many years it was used for house parties by the young people.

When cotton was planted on the island, the slaves were sent over from St. Helena in large row boats to work the land.

Some years ago, the island was bought by a group of developers. A magnificent, new bridge has been built across the inlet from Hunting Island. A canal and beautiful lots have been laid off. A golf course is nearly completed and the developers plan, in the near future, a yacht basin, marinas, air strip, country club and modern shopping center. The beach is one of the finest on the coast and the island is in the heart of the best fishing available.

PRITCHARD ISLAND

Pritchard, an adjoining island, has been purchased as a private estate.

PINCKNEY ISLAND

Nearby Pinckney Island belonged to the Charles Cotesworth Pinckney family. During the Confederate War it was sold for taxes.

Mr. William Elliott wrote in 1859 that Pinckney's "mansion house no longer exists; it was swept away in one of the fearful hurricanes that vex our coast! To this spot, that sterling patriot and lion-hearted soldier retired from the arena of political strife, to spend the evening of his days in social enjoyment and literary relaxation.

"On a small island, jutting out into the bay, affording a delightful view of the ocean, he fixed his residence! There, in the midst of forests of oak, laurel and palmetto, the growth of centuries, his mansion house was erected. There stood the laboratory, with its apparatus for chemical experiments; the library, stored with works of science in various tongues; there bloomed the nursery for exotics; and there was found each other appliance with which taste and intelligence surrounded the abodes of wealth. . . .

"He built where trees of a century's growth gave promise of stability; but . . . among the shifting sands of our coast, old channels are closed, and new ones worn, by prevailing winds and currents . . . during the storms of the equinox, with a force nothing can resist."

For years afterward, the owners of Pinckney Island had it cultivated, but the family did not replace the fine mansion house.

CAPERS ISLAND

Capers Island, across Moon Inlet, from Pritchard's Island, is now being developed. It was purchased recently by Mr. J. E. McTeer and his associates, "Cisca Corporation." A hundred ocean-front lots will be sold.

In the long ago, according to Mr. McTeer, Capers Island was a hunting and fishing ground for the Yemassee Indians. Here are found mounds of old oyster shells, where they "set up the family tepee and held the original oyster roasts."

The developers plan few restrictions for the little island— mainly health and sanitary measures and one house to a lot.

No bridge will connect the place with the numerous nearby islands. It will be a place of privacy, where one can find quiet and relaxation with family and friends.

The developers have ordered a cruiser to take sightseers and prospective buyers around the island, and they hope to start immediately on the construction of homes.

OTHER BARRIER ISLANDS

There are many other barrier islands around Beaufort. Some of these still bear the name of their original owners. This often leads to confusion for the outsider. Today, some of the smaller islands are uninhabited; others have only a few residents—but each might have its own interesting history if we only knew it.

Invasion

BEAUFORT was invaded by Union soldiers in early winter, 1861. This writer realizes that an impartial account of the event could only be accomplished by one who is capable of looking at this great drama of human emotion calmly and disinterestedly.

Rather than recount the story from a possibly biased point of view, I shall endeavor to present both sides: the invasion seen through the eyes of two northern officers; and two southern women.

I

Colonel William Watts Hart Davis was from Doylestown, Pennsylvania. In 1866 he wrote of his stay in Beaufort: "I found Beaufort a beautiful town even under adverse circumstances. It was considered the 'Newport of the South,' and families of wealth resorted to it from the main land of

South Carolina, and from the adjoining states to spend the summer months. It was the seat of elegance, refinement and hospitality.

"On Sunday evening I received an order to steam up to Beaufort, ten miles from Hilton Head. We did not leave until late the next day and reached Beaufort about sundown. The river flows among the islands, on the left washing Lady's Island and St. Helena. We passed but few buildings and saw little evidence of cultivation.

"A few miles below Beaufort we passed the camp of the 1st. South Carolina Volunteers, a Negro regiment being organized by Colonel Thomas W. Higgins, under the auspices of General Saxton. These African defenders of our national honor were lounging about camp and shore, clad in their blue dress coats and scarlet breeches. Our men gazed at them with strange interest, as it was the first time they had ever seen Negroes equipped as soldiers.

"The sight carried me back to an earlier period in the history of the war, when arming Negroes to make soldiers of them dared not be talked about out loud. The first official person connected with the administration of the government who broached this policy was the honorable Simon Cameron, then Secretary of War, but neither the Cabinet nor president at that time dared avow it publicly.

"One evening . . . I was the guest at the home of Colonel Forney, in Washington City, on the occasion of a complimentary supper to George D. Prentice, editor of the *Louisville Journal*. At the supper Mr. Cameron made a few remarks, in which he took ground in favor of arming the Negroes and putting them in the field as soldiers. The idea at that time met with no favor and there is no better judge of this than the fact that the reporter was requested not to mention it in his notice of the occasion . . .

"I have a distinct recollection of the effect it had upon the company. It produced a chilling sensation upon the festive scene. . . ."

(110)

"The town is laid out with regularity, the streets of good width, generally crossing each other at right angles, and shaded with magnificent live oaks and other ornamental trees. The houses are mostly frame, with grounds attached planted with orange and lemon trees, and flowers and shrubbery which, in their dilapidation, gave evidence of having been tastily laid out.

"The 'Green' of several acres is shaded with live oaks. . . . The town has been but little injured by military occupation.

"The sound of Admiral DuPont's guns at Hilton Head gave great alarm to the inhabitants at Beauford (Beaufort). Its fall was wholly unexpected for they (the citizens) had been led to believe that the forts were impregnable. Therefore, when they learned they had been taken, they were panic-stricken, and fled in dismay. Their departure was hurried. They did not take time to pack up, but left everything standing. Needlework was found lying on the table where it was thrown when the alarm first sounded; dresses and other articles of wardrobe in closet and drawer; silver plate and elegant china in the sideboard, and books on their shelves. Every appliance of domestic and social life was abandoned.

"They hastened across the island to Port Royal ferry, where they crossed over to the main land.

"The Negroes commenced to pillage before the Army arrived, and when it landed, the victorious heroes were received by wenches dressed in silks and satins that had adorned the beautiful forms of Carolina's fairest daughters.

"The plunder was not all obtained by soldiers, but officers received a fair share! Their conduct in this particular was disgraceful, and should have cost the offending ones their commissions. Some of them sent North pianos, elegant furniture, silver ware, books, pictures, etc., to adorn their New England dwellings. Most of the troops that formed the DuPont-Sherman expedition were from that section of the country. Beaufort was a garrison town the rest of the war, and the point where the general hospitals were located.

(111)

"The 104th regiment was never more comfortable than when at Beaufort. The camp on the village green was within a hundred yards of the river.

"While stationed at Beaufort, I was invited to go into the country to witness a Negro praise meeting and wedding on a warm Sunday morning in June. A ride of a few miles brought us to the place—a plantation that belonged to a clergyman of the name of Walker. Several ladies and gentlemen were assembled, some from adjoining plantations and others from town. The religious services were held in the cotton house, conducted by a Mr. Conant, an ex-officer of a Maine regiment. The bride was a plantation girl and the groom a soldier of Montgomery's regiment.

"The room was cleared for the praise meeting in which church members only participated. They formed themselves in a circle around the room, all standing. Three men, seated on a bench at one side, now commenced a chant which increased in violence as they proceeded when the worshippers began to move around the room, keeping hold of hands. They kept time to the music with their bodies and limbs, and repeated the words of the refrain. Sometimes they moved backward—sometimes forward, and sometimes sideways, all the while wiggling and twisting their bodies into many attitudes, shuffling their feet to time, and beating the cadence with their hands.

"The music of the chant was wild melancholy, and monotonous, but not entirely devoid of harmony. Sometimes the voices would swell into a loud and full chorus, then sink again to a whisper, but at no time did they reach the shouting pitch. The leader of the three singers changed the words and the tune at pleasure, apparently impromptu and without method. His hands were kept in lively motion and his actions reminded one of a darkie beating Juba. At one time refrain had some application to boating, when the Negroes, as they swept round the room in measured cadence, worked their arms as though pulling at the oar. The dances of some of our western Indian tribes is not unlike what I witnessed. It was evidently a heathen ceremony handed down from their African ancestors, somewhat modified by their Christian training.

"The young ladies living at one of the Barnwell plantations, a few miles from Beaufort, gave a picnic to their friends one fine summer afternoon, where I was invited to be a guest and help enjoy the fun. The spot was delightful. The dwelling was situated far within the embrace of the pine wood, and near one of the numerous watercourses that divide the islands. Around it was the finest grove of venerable live oaks that I have ever seen. The place selected for dancing was under a natural arbor formed by the intervening branches overhead. It seemed to me more than passing strange that a man could be willing to relinquish such a home as this one and join his fortunes to a rebellion against his government and country. Such men must have been earnest in their course and believed themselves in the right."

* * * *

Colonel Davis evidently attended the praise meeting on Retreat Plantation and the picnic at "Woodward," Colonel Robert Barnwell's plantation.

Colonel Davis, who seemed to be quite taken with Beaufort, had some remarks to make about "do-gooders" and Negroes, as follows:

"Beaufort was headquarters of the humanitarian side of the war. It was the center of the operation of the 'Freedmen's Society,' an institution organized in New England for the ostensible purpose of ameliorating the condition of the Negro.

"Schools were established on all the islands within our lines, where Yankee school marms taught the young Africans . . . While men fought the master, the women tried to civilize the slave and with but *indifferent* success . . . The laborers in the vineyard were known as 'Gideonites,' where head and front was Reverend Mr. French who found that *the war paid him better than peace.*

"General Saxton was nominally at the head of the organization . . . The deserted plantations were given to the 'Gideonites'."

Much later in the war, Davis was again sent to the islands . . .

"On my return I found the men of the 104th Pennsylvania very much incensed against General Birney. Soon after he assumed command of the District, he issued an order to compel the Negroes to come in from the neighboring plantations to work on the fortification being erected on Hilton Head. At the same time he ordered a detail of six men from my regiment to cook for these Negroes . . .

"This detail was made from a white regiment at a time two Negro regiments were encamped near where the work was to be done. There could have been no other motive than to *degrade* the white soldier and insult the regiment. That these men of the 104th were not obliged to cook the victuals of the South Carolina Negroes was no fault of General Birney. Is it then a cause of wonder that he was heartily *hated* by the white troops?

"The first of June, Colonel Montgomery, with his Negro regiment, made a raid up the Combahee River on the Main Land to get recruits. They embarked on two armed steamboats at Beaufort. So far as recruiting was concerned the expedition was quite a success. He brought back some eight hundred darkies of all ages and conditions . . . They seemed better fitted to hoe cotton than carry a musket. There may be a difference between stealing Negroes from their home on the Congo, in Africa, to hoe cotton and cane, and stealing them from the Combahee in South Carolina to compel them to perform an involuntary and disliked service, but many people do not see the difference."

II
(Extracts from Captain Marple's Letters)

Captain Alfred Marple wrote his wife in a letter date-lined April 30th . . .

"We are having delightful weather. Sometimes, however, it is very hot in the middle of the day but the evenings are always pleasant, and we can set under the shades of the spreading oaks until midnight without getting uncomfortably cool . . .

"There is a species of tree here now out in bloom that I have never seen before. It is the pomegranate, very beautiful, large, and red and scarlet. There is another larger tree, called 'Pride of China,' which looks very much like our lilacs, that is the flowers. Oleanders are very common in the yards and grow from eight to fourteen feet, they are now coming into bloom, but they are nothing in comparison with the pomegranate flower in point of beauty. Roses and verbena are in every yard and decorate many of the graves in the churchyard."

And another, May 26, 1863 . . .

"We are feasting on dewberries everyday, using them three times a day. The briers hang with them in ropes. Wild plums are also very plenty and ripe."

May 31, 1863 . . .

"We are still idling here, and I think the prospect of our being transferred to some other post is rather faint. General Rufus Saxon has command of the troops here, and is Military Governor of 'this and the surrounding islands' . . . Colonel Saxon [1] was married since our arrival here to a Miss

---

[1] General Rufus Saxton, known as the "Deliverer," was originator of the Freedmen's Bureau in South Carolina and began the campaign for "Forty Acres and a Mule" for Negroes. He was succeeded in January, 1866, by General R. K. Scott who was less ardent in his advocacy of Negro rights and held a more conciliatory attitude toward owners and former occupants of the lands. First attempt to put Negroes in charge of lands was the sale March, 1863, when forty-seven plantations were sold, six

Thompson, she formerly lived in Bucks County, and she was engaged in teaching Negroes at the time she made the General's acquaintance. She is quite pretty, with auburn hair, and is smart and lively. She resides with him in the largest and prettiest house in the town . . ."

May 31, 1863 . . .

"I witnessed the marriage of a discharged soldier this evening, to a mulatto woman, that could not at the North be detected as having Negro blood in her veins. I do not like this mixing up of races, which God intended should be kept separate, and it brings a curse with it as their children, if they have any, will curse their memory . . ."

June 30, 1863 . . .

". . . I hope I may be placed on Ladys Island for pickett duty, as it is a very pleasant place and the Sound is well stocked with fish. Young sharks are very abundant and are good eating. The figs are not yet ripe, but soon will be. They were over ripe this time last year."

Soon after this, Captain Marple's regiment left for Folly Island.

III

When Miss Emily Barnwell Walker died some years ago at the age of eighty-seven, she left a written account of her family's departure from Beaufort:

"In November, 1861, General Dunavant's regiment was camped on the edge of town. Not long afterwards, a rumor came that the Yankees had made up a big fleet to capture Charleston or Beaufort. Every man under sixty was at the forts—Bay Point, Hilton Head and another nearer Beau-

---

only going to Negroes who could buy them, and the rest to Northerners. On January 15, 1865, General W. T. Sherman issued his famous "Field Order No. 15" reserving for Negroes the sea islands from Charleston, taking in those bordering the St. John's River, plus all abandoned rice fields for thirty miles from the sea.

(Continued on page 133)

Fort Frederick, beautifully kept, is located on the grounds of the United States Naval Hospital. An outstanding example of tabby, its now-crumbling walls reveal whole oyster shells. The Fort, on the Beaufort River between the Town of Beaufort and Port Royal Sound, was erected for protection against the Indians, and the Spaniards who sailed their galleons up the river. It is downstream from Spanish Point.

The Fripp House—now Tid-alholm—presented a different appearance during the Confederate War. This property also once belonged to the Haskells before coming into possession of the Rowland family.

Tidalholm was built in the 1850's by Edgar Fripp, wealthy landowner, for a summer home. In the 1860's, when the house was sold for taxes, it was purchased by an anonymous Frenchman, who presented it as a present to the family. He then vanished, leaving no name or address.

Picturesqueness and variety reach perfection at Bluffton on the River May. Many summer homes are built on the high bluff from which the town derives its name. Great mounds of oyster shells cover the foreground, providing natural launches for fishermen's boats.

An old Beaufort County rice field points up one of the principal industries of long ago. Rice gate in foreground is now used to flood field, today a wild life preserve. Pegs are placed in various holes, raising or lowering gate to control flow of water.

This old Verdier house, with its high fence and unique gates, was used by the United States Sanitary Commission, 1862-65. At one time a Rhett house, it is now known as "Marshlands."

"Marshlands" is the home of Mr. and Mrs. Sterling Harris, who have lived in Beaufort since the 1940's. The home, built by James Verdier in 1814, has a fine Adams mantel in its drawing room.

The Baptist Church of Beaufort.

Beaufort College is now a branch of the University of South Carolina. In 1795 a group of Beaufort citizens obtained a charter for the college's establishment, which was to be supported by the sale of vacant lots in the town and from the sale of escheated and confiscated property in the Parish. Previous to the opening of Beaufort College, sons in the ante-bellum period were sent to the College of Charleston, Harvard, Princeton and Yale.

(121)

The Christensen House, typical of the lowcountry, is set on a high, gracefully-arched brick basement. The yard, planted by Neils Christensen, Sr., has a wealth of native flowers and unusual shrubs. The house, said to have been erected about 1805-06, was purchased by Mr. Christensen in 1881. Originally built as a Methodist Parsonage for a Mr. Ledbetter, the home in later years was owned by the Reverend Stephen Elliott and in the 1850's by Dr. Louis DeSassure.

Tabby Manse, with its perfectly proportioned upper and lower porches and low roof, is two stories high and has a basement. It was built by Thomas Fuller some time after 1786 and is one of the older houses in Beaufort. Now owned by Miss Alma Greenwood, it was once in the possession of Mr. Onthank, operator of the Sea Island Hotel.

The Paul Hamilton House— now "The Oaks"—was Hospital No. 1 during the occupation of Beaufort by Federal Forces. Copy from faded photograph shows patients and officers on upper and lower porches.

"The Oaks," appropriately named for the large trees in the beautifully landscaped yard, is the home of Mr. and Mrs. Paul Schwartz. This house was built by Paul Hamilton, grandson of Paul Hamilton of the same name, who was Secretary of the Navy under President Madison (1806-13), Comptroller of the State of South Carolina (1799-1800) and Governor of South Carolina (1804-06). It has also been known as a Fuller House. A delightful little ghost story tells of a tiny lady who used to appear at intervals to warn the residents in time of danger. Quite often she was seen sitting on the stairs, where she would let no one pass until the danger was over.

Provost Marshall's Office

On right, Dr. Master's store; next to it, Customs' House

Store For Freedmen, Beaufort

Home of the Lockwoods in which they operated a bank.

Recent renovations to this lovely home on The Point disclosed features indicating it was built in the late eighteenth century. In the mid-nineteenth century it was extensively re-modeled by George Morse Stoney. It is presently owned and occupied by Mr. Roscoe Mitchell and Mrs. Mitchell, who was a Pollitzer, former family owners. The interior is particularly interesting and authentically furnished.

The John Trask House on the Bay

Old White Church on St. Helena now stands in ruins. The tabby structure was erected as a Chapel of Ease to St. Helena Parish at Beaufort and is located a short distance from the Penn Community House. The chapel, dating from about 1794, was destroyed in a forest fire and never rebuilt.

This perfectly preserved fortification, hidden by overgrowths of myrtle and vines, is on St. Helena Island. A relic of the Spanish-American War, Fort Fremont was named for John Charles Fremont, a native South Carolinian. Fremont, a controversial figure of the Confederate War era, was the first Republican candidate for the presidency of the United States. He is known best historically as the "Pathfinder of the West," from explorations opening up land routes from the Mississippi to the West Coast.

The William Hilton Inn

Remains of gun emplacement are a curiosity to visitors at Hilton Head. Around 1900, America's first and only steam gun was erected on Port Royal Sound, near Confederate Fort Walker, and after one attempt at firing the gun, the innovation in warfare was abandoned. The gun—in that erratic performance—set fire to vegetation on Bay Point Island.

Gateway to the Sea Islands from Town of Beaufort.

Sailing! One of Beaufort's favorite amusements!

Fripp Island Bridge, joining the resort to Hunting Island.

The Fripp Mansion is the home of Dr. and Mrs. Marshall C. Sanford of Pompano Beach, Florida. Its exquisite interior contains elaborate cornices and carved woodwork. Mural landscapes done in oils are painted above the Adams mantels in the parlor and drawing room.

Coffin Point, built in 1809, is the home of Mr. and Mrs. J. E. McTeer. The plantation of Thomas A. Coffin, on which it was situated, was said to be the best managed on St. Helena Island. When the house was vacated at the time of the Invasion of Beaufort, its furniture included handsome rosewood tables, sideboards and washstands with marble tops. The Coffin trademark was a "pinch-toe" coffin. Senator Cameron of Pennsylvania was a former owner.

The Hunting Island Lighthouse affords a panoramic view of the surrounding Sea Islands and the Atlantic Ocean. Built in 1873, the Lighthouse cast its 120,000 candlepower beam to seamen, before being abandoned. It is interesting to tourists who enjoy climbing its iron, spiraling stairway. A glistening coat of white paint conceals a cast-iron body bolted together in sections. The tower—moved from several locations—is a landmark for boating parties traveling the Intracoastal Waterway from St. Helena Sound to Port Royal Sound.

The remains of Sheldon Church in Prince William's Parish stand today as they did shortly after the Revolutionary War. The beautiful church was burned in 1780 when the British under General Prevost passed it on their march from Savannah to the seige of Charles Town. It was rebuilt after that war and suffered destruction again during the Confederate War. In 1864 it was used as a stable by Sherman's troops, the torch again being applied. While it stood as a ruin following the Revolution, Charles Fraser, the noted miniaturist, painted it. His watercolor, with thirty-nine other lowcountry scenes, is included in "A Charleston Sketchbook."

A copy of an old brochure shows lithograph of water scene in front of old Sea Island Hotel. Pleasure boats of all descriptions, including sail and covered canoes, were provided for guests. Dock reached from shore to bath house (right foreground). Upper part was used as a bandstand for concerts for guests who listened to good music while lounging on grass-covered banks of the Bay. The hotel at this time was operated by Mr. and Mrs. A. F. Odell.

The Sea Island Motel—overlooking the Bay—is on the site of the old Sea Island Hotel from which it takes its name. Gathering place of society, the old Hotel became a famous spa, with a cuisine noted for exotic dishes. Today, the restaurant of the Sea Island Motel is also gaining a reputation for its unusual cuisine, especially sea food. Its recipe for She-Crab Soup is requested so frequently that the management keeps printed copies by the cash register.

fort. Saturday, I went around to Grandma's. Aunt Sarah Barnwell decided she would pack up the books. Daddy Will, the butler, brought the boxes in and we filled them—he nailed them up.

"On Sunday a despatch from General Ripley saying all who would like to leave town by water, must do so before Monday, as the fleet had sailed for Beaufort. The battle, he thought, would be fought on Monday!

"The women decided they would take no chances of being shut up on this island with Yankees. I went around to Grandma's to see what they were going to do. Grandma was born in exile in Maryland when we were fighting our ancestors, the English. Her father was a nephew of Governor Bull who had been appointed by King George.

"General Tarleton was furious with him for going against his King. He sent word to her father and told him, 'When I come to your estate, a crow [2] will have to take its rations along in its flight across.'

"So my Grandma's father sent his family and one hundred slaves to Maryland.

"Grandma was now eighty-two. She, Aunts Sarah and Emily, decided that on account of Grandma's age, they would leave at once. The coachman, Daddy Sam, was told to drive the carriage to the front door as the Yankee fleet was coming and there would be a fight Monday."

" 'Make my Missus leave her home!' he exclaimed."

Miss Walker's story continued, "Daddy Sam was Maum Clarinda's brother. They were a family of Negroes my grandfather thought highly of. It was a big yard. Grandma kept thirty Negroes in it, big and little, to work in and around the house.

---

[2] This statement is also credited to Sherman in his future treatment of South Carolina, made before his "March to the Sea."

"Now, without a white man in sight, those Negroes made up a bed on a stretcher for Grandma, looking heartbroken as they worked. There was no talking by anyone except what was absolutely necessary.

"My Grandma, Sarah Bull Barnwell, sat in a chair. Daddy Will took it up on one side and Daddy Sam on the other. In solemn silence they carried her out to the carriage and tenderly placed her on a pallet. My two aunts and a maid, Maum Tenah, entered the carriage. Another maid got up on the coach beside Daddy Sam. The foot boy put up the steps and took his place on the little seat at the back of the carriage, and Daddy Sam drove away. Grandma never saw her home again.

"That evening I went to church alone. A little bird flew in. Around and around it went. I was feeling bad enough before, and that almost put an end to my self control. The old Negroes had filled me with superstitions, but *didn't they come right?*

"Papa [3] got home from his church across the river about dark. Mama insisted that we must leave. Daddy Jimmy was sent out to Retreat Plantation to order the boat 'Santa Anna' brought in immediately. How the Negroes accomplished it, I don't know. But by nine o'clock the boat with its six oarsmen had anchored in front of the town. They said they were awfully hungry, but were willing to wait until they had rowed a certain distance, as the tide was about to turn.

"They carried a mattress and placed it in the bottom of the boat, jerked up a carpet and threw that over the awning and three trunks. We carried a pot and food for the Negroes to cook. We had three Negro women and six Negro men aboard. My father steered. A lantern was placed on top of the awning to keep other boats from running into us.

"As soon as we could, we stopped to let the Negroes cook. We drew up to shore—these six black men around us and

---

[3] A minister.

the black night—it did look weird—this boat with its white women and children, and one white man.

"Before we landed in the morning, the battle had begun. We heard the shells explode in the water. Grandma was at my uncle's home, 'The Briars,' to receive us. Daddy Will arrived next day with two boat loads of furniture from Grandma's house.

"He went back immediately and succeeded in bringing two more boatloads. Maumer's husband came up to say all the Negroes on Retreat Plantation were at the landing. Papa told them to go back and share out the corn. Maumer with her husband and children came on to the house, Maumer protesting, 'Go back? I ain't leaving my missus, where she go, I go'.

"A few weeks later, Sarah Bull Barnwell died in Walterboro where she had been carried to be farther away from the firing. Her great-granddaughter wrote, '. . . and here in Walterboro, she died . . . as she had been born, in exile.' No one knows but those who have passed through the experience what sadness *that* word implies."

IV

Mrs. Randolph Sams of Beaufort wrote several letters to her husband from Barnwell where she was refugeeing, regarding the invasion.

As the great war was nearing its end, on February 3, 1865, only two weeks before Columbia was surrendered to the Federal Army, a letter came from Barnwell, South Carolina . . . "My Own Darling R—,

"Mrs. Pope has just arrived from Allendale in great alarm as the Yankees were skirmishing with our men just six miles below that place. Poor thing, like many others, she leaves most of her effects to fall into their grasp. Annie Pope has been staying with us but left on the arrival of her sister. They now occupy Colonel Hulson's house."

"Feb. 5th—Kanapaux' Battery passed through the town long before dawn of the day, on the retreat which roused us from our troubled slumber as our men told us that the Battery would be removed if the General concluded not to make a stand. I woke the children and put on them two suits of underclothing and their dresses and wore the same quantity myself, besides three small bags containing needles, cotton and flax thread, tape and buttons. I am a burthen to myself, but must try to save a few articles.

"Pa carried most of my money, and my jewelry is concealed, also your important papers. My room looks more like a commissary room than a bedroom.

"Many of Wheeler's Command are here and report says the Yankees are nine miles off this evening. They are expected in town tomorrow. Pa went as far as Blackville yesterday but returned today on important business—he just left for the same place again. Another anxious night before us. This continued suspense and anxiety causes me to feel nervous and badly. God bless and keep you all is my prayer."

"Feb. 6th—Ma has just sent me to ask some gentlemen who are standing by this house if there were any reliable reports current . . . they say the Yankees are reported to be about eight miles off but he thought they will not come in today, but if they are so near why should they postpone their march when they will meet with no resistance?

"One wounded man is in our piazza, the poor fellow is wounded in three places and has a hot fever, but he will not recline in the parlor, as it will cause him too much pain to ascend the steps. Bet has just made him some lemonade, which he says refreshed him very much.

"Our troops are retreating steadily now. They have carried the wounded off on horseback. The Yankees are just beyond the limits of the town. Great God, deliver us from the hands of this fiendish foe!"

"Feb. 8th—The Yankees came into town yesterday at

two o'clock, fired at some of our men who remained to see them enter. We were on our piazza at the time, but the balls struck none of us. They pursued our men across the creek but found it a fruitless errand, so returned.

"They kept marching in, right in front of our house till I thought that the division must have comprised the whole Yankee and foreign nations. Eight thousand cavalry passed before dark. It was Kilpatrick's Division. They had not all marched in before the stable in Cousin Bet's yard, which contained Pa's carriage and Cousin F's buggy, was fired, and in half an hour after Louisa and her little ones were turned into the streets.

"They next fired Wm. deTreville's office, the Ivestman's store, the Fergusons' barn, which caught his house. The Grahams' fine house was also burned. Mrs. Oakman screamed when the Yankees rode up the street. I could but feel that it was best to remain firm as possible. I've found it very difficult to keep the children from giving vent to their feelings, but after some reasoning, they have become more calm.

"One of the first twenty went into our house. Of course asked if any Rebels were in the house. Finally they took their departure but we were not allowed to remain in quiet for long, for two came in very soon after, and after catechising me as the first did, asked what kind of treatment we expected at their hands. I replied that we always expected civil and polite treatment from gentlemen. He said *there were no gentlemen in the Yankee Army,* as it was entirely composed of convicts released for the purpose of subjugating the rebellion.

"Ma then said she would expect the officer to treat us as Ladies should be. 'You will find the officers worse than the men,' he said. My strength surely had been given me by an Almighty Power and could not be taken from me by a Yankee's venomous tongue. We were all nervous but to all appearance perfectly calm.

"Just as we had gotten rid of those, two others stole up the back steps, got into my room and were searching everywhere; at the same time others had broken into our cellar door, stealing our molasses. I could stand it no longer, so got Bet to accompany me to headquarters (Mrs. Brown's house) where I succeeded in getting a guard. An officer (Lieutenant Fuler) accompanied us home. He made the two men return all they took from me. One of them seemed quite sulky and told him that before night 'she would have nothing left.' The guard tried all in his power to keep the men out, but there were sometimes ten in the house and yard, killing our poultry and stealing from the Negroes.

"They fired Sid Brown's store twice, and each time we went for an officer and had it extinguished he made them promise not to do it again. But they went directly off and fired Mr. Aldrich's office and the Masonic Hall which very soon caught the Browns' store and in an hour after, we were turned out into the street in all the cold and rain . . ."

"Feb. 14—A rumor is rife this morning that the Yankees are but six miles from here, but few seem to believe it, as I had just heard that they are at least eighteen miles and will not probably reach here before tomorrow, but reports are so contradictory that they may come upon the town before we are aware of it. Bet, Ma and myself have been busy all day removing our provisions from the cellar and pantry into our bedrooms, hoping they may be more secure. It was fatiguing after having sat up more than half the night making bread and biscuits for Lewis and Pa to take with them.

"We emptied the cotton out of one of our mattresses and filled it nicely with all of our cloth, sheets, blankets and men's clothing. Sewed it up like a mattress and put it under the rest. Whether they discover it will be proved by tomorrow, I fear. Pa and Lewis start for Lexington District to remain until the Yankees pass through.

Looking Backward

I

AROUND old Beaufort Town for many years have ebbed the tides of war and peace. Her sons have gone forth to battle. Some returned crowned with glory—others sacrificed their lives for what they considered right and just.

In the peacetime of 1857, Captain George Elliott wrote of some of Beaufort's distinguished sons: Thomas Heyward, signer of the Declaration of Independence and judge of South Carolina; Robert Barnwell, speaker of the House of Representatives and member of Congress; Stephen Elliott, botanist and first editor of the *Southern Review;* Edward Dewar Simons, professor of marked ability; John A. Stuart, gloriously gifted genius and brilliant editor of *The Charleston Mercury;* William J. Grayson, poet; R. Barnwell Rhett; the Reverend John Elliott, D.D., first-honor graduate of South Carolina College.

To those who have called the old town home, her name is sweeter than the finest music; and the memory of the perfume of her roses, the frou-frouing of the palms in the breeze, the moonlight on the Bay, the sunshine filtering through the moss, and ancient oaks resting on the old homes, are treasured in their hearts, though land and sea may separate them from her.

Diaries and pictures record the fact that in 1759 Beaufort consisted of about thirty houses. Some of these can be recognized in Campbell's painting of that year, a copy of which hangs in the public library at Beaufort. It was probably about this period that Beaufort's first streets were named.

We were British subjects, so "King Street" was named in honor of His Royal Highness. A little son was born to Her Majesty and the next street was called "Prince." Then, there was "Duke"—giving honor not only to the next in line of royal importance, but also because Beaufort was named for the Duke of Beaufort.

About this time a law was passed that "all persons taking up front lots must build thereon in three years and on back lots in four years." With the clouds of the Revolutionary War hanging heavy over them, and afterwards, the long, dreary years of fighting when the British entered the town, there was no thought given to enlarging it or enforcing the street law.

When the Revolution was over and America was a free and independent nation, Beaufort thought it time to expand. So another street was opened, "Washington," named for George Washington, because he won the war. Next came "Greene Street," because Nathanael Greene helped George win. "Greene" was followed by "Congress" to commemorate the first Congress. Last was "Boundary"—because Beaufort decided she just didn't want to grow any more!

II

Johnson in his "Reminiscences" relates a traditional story of the nearby countryside, that occurred before the Revolution. He calls it "Bloody Point:"

The islands of Port Royal and St. Helena were fairly thickly inhabited by white settlers, while the neighboring islands, Hilton Head, Daufuski and Pinckney, were held in possession by a few scattered Indians who formed a kind of neutral ground between the white and red men.

The Georgia Indians were in the habit of making frequent forays on the Carolina settlements, killing the inhabitants and carrying off in boats whatever plunder they collected to their homes farther south. Large war parties were sometimes formed who would proceed to Hilton Head and skulk in the thickets until a fair chance offered, when they would cross over Broad River and ravage the neighborhood. Hence

(140)

was derived the name of "Skulk" Creek—not "Skull" as it is now generally called and placed on maps.

After these invasions, the Indians would return to Skulk Creek with their plunder, to elude pursuit amongst its numerous thickets and windings. After one of these expeditions, having committed a number of murders and loaded their canoes, they never halted until they reached the end of Daufuskie, where they supposed themselves safe. A very strong party of whites set out in pursuit of them. On reaching Hilton Head, they learned from some friendly Indians that their enemies had proceeded farther south. Inducing these friendly Indians to join them as guides, the party continued the pursuit.

When the men reached Daufuskie, they discovered the smoke of the Indian Camp, where they had halted on the end of that island. The whites and their guides landed on the northwest portion and marched toward their enemies. The Indians had put all of their boats a short distance up the river to avoid the surf which breaks upon the point, and there at its extremity, were enjoying the good things which they had stolen. The white men approached cautiously, until passing between the Indians and their canoes, effectually cut off the savages' retreat. A shower of bullets was the first information received by the Indians of the presence of any enemy.

The surprise was complete—the massacre dreadful—the white sand crimson with blood. Some escaped by swimming, but nearly all of the Indian party was killed. Forever afterward, the place where the fighting occurred, has been known as "Bloody Point."

III

Beaufort College had been chartered in 1795; and the wealthy planters' sons attended it prior to finishing their education at Harvard, Yale, Princeton or in Europe.

Girls had private governesses and tutors. They were well versed in music, languages, the art of dancing and entering a room gracefully. Later they would spend a year or two at a school for young ladies in Charleston or at some other equally desirable place. For several decades many private schools catering to the daughters of wealthy and socially prominent families sprang up in the South.

In the heyday of indigo, rice and cotton, the planters built large, airy houses at Beaufort and furnished them in the luxurious manner of their English forebears. The houses were overflowing with servants and the owners entertained with lavishness and elegance. The women and children often spent part of the summer at a famous resort. They would arrive in style with carriage, coachman and personal maids and nurses.

Simple houses, except in some instances, such as the Fripp House and Coffin Point on St. Helena, were constructed on the plantations. From these places the work of the plantation was directed.

An Agricultural Society was formed—having other interests besides planting. At these meetings, politics of the day were discussed and at times a bit of scandal crept in. The meetings usually ended with a course dinner and plenty of refreshments.

IV

William John Grayson (1788-1863) was born in Beaufort. In his diary—a copy of which is in the Beaufort Library—he wrote of a Hunting Club in Beaufort. One of the rules of the club was that no man was allowed to go home sober! Mr. Grayson tells of two instances of visitors having objected to the rule. One of the stories is given: "A young Scotsman, Robert Brown, lately come to Beaufort to engage in mercantile business with Mr. Mair, was invited to the club. After a reasonable time, Mr. Brown refused another drink. The members of the club insisted and still Mr. Brown objected. The dispute waxed warm. At last it was proposed that it be settled by a race. Mr. Brown was to have a five-yard start. If any member of the club could catch him, he was to submit to the laws of the club—if he outran them, he was to do as he pleased. Word was given and Mr. Brown outran them."

Others tell that after that night Beaufort knew Mr. Brown no more.

V

Years ago, the Agricultural Society held one of its meetings a few miles out of Beaufort at "Oak Point Plantation". After the meeting and its accompanying dinner that lasted for two hours, the gentlemen "socialized" for another two.

The last of the planters to depart was an intimate friend and relative of the host, who walked him out to mount his horse. Before this planter rode away, his friend gave him a package to take home, saying, "Here is a bottle of the finest Irish peat whiskey. Keep it for some special occasion."

The man rode only a short distance home before he said to himself, "Since this is such excellent whiskey, I believe I'll just taste it." So he reined in his horse and took a sip or two.

The night was cold and in a little while he took several more sips out of the bottle. Then asking himself what was the use of keeping the whiskey since it had already been opened, he took a long drink.

He was approaching Whale Branch, which at this time had only a narrow, single-passage, wooden bridge to span it. As he drew nearer, there came the sound of many steps passing over the loose boards. Dismounting, the planter pulled his horse to one side. In a few moments an enormous camel loomed before his startled eyes. Scarcely before he could catch his breath, a huge elephant followed, the moonlight causing its small, cunning eyes to shine like balls of fire. Trembling, he held on to his horse for assurance. But when there came the rattling of wheels and the unmistakable roar of a lion, the planter sank to his knees and then and there, took the pledge. It was never broken.

The explanation for the phenomena of the night, of course, was simple. A small, wandering circus had been stranded in Beaufort. The owner, having run up a lot of debts, was slipping out of town after dark so that his creditors could not confiscate his show animals!

* * * *

Out of the past, also, comes the tale of the Barbecue House, on the edge of the river, beyond where the courthouse now stands. No lady was allowed inside the doors of the Barbecue House, because here the men met to play chess and poker and drink. In the storm of 1805, the house was washed away.

Professor Lindley, a teacher at Beaufort College, wrote a sensational poem, "The Fall of The Barbecue House," describing the shenanigans, following its destruction. For this, he was discharged from the college. So . . . that being the case . . . perhaps it is best to let the poem lie in its dusty archives, and not repeat it here.

VI

During the war, a kindly, short, bow-legged man named A. F. Odell came along with the Union Army to Hilton Head as a baker. In the fall of 1865, now being in Beaufort, he opened his own bakery shop in the pretentious Habersham House on the Bay. His wife, Rosalie, died some time thereafter and was buried in a corner of St. Helena churchyard.

The man was lonely and he had his little son, Bennie, to provide for. It was difficult for a man to work all day and at the same time see after a child. Unfortunately, in Beaufort at the time there were few eligible, unmarried ladies, except those who had come down from the North to teach the Negroes, and these women were not interested in the baker.

Becoming desperate, he decided to advertise in a northern newspaper for a wife. In that part of the country, glowing stories of lovely homes and capable servants had preceded his advertisement, so when Miss Alice Clancy read it, the romance of the situation appealed to her. Realizing that she was not getting any younger and that many eligible men had been killed in the war, she wrote the baker a letter. After a brief correspondence with her proposed husband, and after having secured several character references from Union officers, Miss Clancy sailed for Beaufort via Charleston, wearing as a wedding gift her mother's expensive coral jewelry.

Changing boats in Charleston, she sailed on to meet her destiny. Her heart sank when she caught the first glimpse of the man she had promised to marry . . . and she felt that she could not keep her promise. She determined then to tell him that she would be returning home. But when she looked down and saw little Bennie, he stretched out his arms to her . . . she changed her mind and sinking down beside him, whispered, "God has sent me to you."

So Miss Alice Clancy became Mrs. A. F. Odell; and the couple was very happy. She worked beside her husband in the bakery shop, and they prospered.

When the Sea Island Hotel was offered for sale by two northerners who had acquired it after the war, the Odells bought it, offering lavish services—including transportation—to their guests.

VII

The house which became the Sea Island Hotel was built by a Scotchman, Dr. Stoney, when he married Elizabeth Barnwell. Later Nathaniel Heyward bought it. (Heyward also owned "White Hall," on the Combahee River, and generally was believed to be the wealthiest man in the District. It was estimated that he owned over two thousand slaves in addition to other property.)

When John Stuart, editor of the newspaper in Beaufort, married Claudia Rhett, he leased the old Stoney House from Heyward. At the close of the war, two men, by the names of Onthank and Kindman, bought this old home. For a time they operated it as the Sea Island Hotel, then it came into the possession of the Odells.

For many years under the Odells' management, the hotel was popular. They built a large annex on the back of the building, crowding it to capacity when United States ships were docked at the port. The 1875 hotel register is as interesting as it is revealing. It contains names of officers from the ships, U. S. S. Dictator, Congress, U. S. S. Catskill, U. S. S. Hartford, and many other names, including the captains and pilots of local boats plying between Charleston and Savannah, such as the Punta, Sunshine and Paune.

At this time, Beaufort and the Sea Islands seemed to be a hotbed of news for northern reporters. C. D. Jenny, correspondent for *The New York World* was frequently registered at the hotel. Representatives from *Harper's Magazine, Harper's Weekly, Outlook,* and other periodicals of the day, seemed to find everything about the places interesting. *The New York Nation* covered Negro life and other activities of the times. All this brought a vast amount of business to the Odells.

One page of the old Sea Island register is filled with names of John Robinson's Circus. Mrs. Robinson always accompanied her husband; she was much younger than he and newspaper articles tell that she was a very handsome woman.

A glance at the register also reveals that the great and near-great of the North and South were guests there. As the hotel became more and more famous, often whole families would come to spend weeks in its pleasant atmosphere.

Traveling men soon learned the best food obtainable was served by the Odells and arranged their schedules to stop in Beaufort as often as possible. The proprietors offered many inducements. In season, oyster roasts and clam bakes for guests were held weekly at Bay Point. There was music each night for dancing and sometimes masquerade balls were held.

A bandstand was erected on the Bay. Here, in the late afternoons, an orchestra played. Underneath the pavilion was a bath house; nearby was a landing where boats docked.

The people of Beaufort admired and respected Mr. and Mrs. Odell. She was particularly loved for her kindness and generosity. One of their children was a girl who grew up to become a famous actress.

The whole family is gone now . . . as is the old Sea Island Hotel.

VIII

Early in the Confederate War a mysterious old lady appeared on Parris Island. She took up her residence in an isolated, abandoned cabin. No one knew anything about her, until later it was learned that she was an important spy for the Federals, reporting personally to President Lincoln.

After the occupation of Hilton Head Island, and the end of the war, her son was in charge of the Freedman's Bureau. He bought one of the fine homes on the Bay at a Tax Sale. It contained a huge bath tub—called by the invaders, "Neopolitanic." The tub was eight feet long and very wide, possibly made on special order for a very tall man. It was carved from one piece of brownish marble and was described as being the color of milk chocolate.

The grandson of the old lady was born in Beaufort and became a respected and wealthy man.

IX

An amusing clipping was revealed among Mrs. Douglas Gregorie's papers. Regretfully, the date and name of the newspaper are missing. It begins, "Old timers tell a story of dignified old Beaufort in the days before the war when some of the Progressives wanted to build a hotel in the town. There was a general protest from the Conventionals.

" 'There was no need for a hotel,' they argued. Their argument, very simple, was that 'If the right people came to Beaufort, they would be entertained in private homes; and if they were the other sort, they were not wanted in Beaufort anyway'!"

X

The McKees were early settlers in Beaufort. More than three decades before the turn of the eighteenth century, land was recorded in their name.

About 1825, John McKee's son, Henry, built a large two-story house on Prince Street in Beaufort, for his bride. Soon afterward, John McKee died and Henry inherited a cotton plantation, called "Ashdale," on Ladies Island. In addition, he was heir to a large number of slaves.

Among these was a woman called "Lydia," and her son, Robert Smalls. Henry McKee's family was especially fond of the two Negroes. Lydia had been with the family when young Henry was born. Her son Robert was an unusually bright boy who was constantly with his master or playing with Henry and the other McKee children.

The McKees had every confidence in Lydia's loyalty, but for many years she had been plotting against them, always with the idea of eventually gaining freedom. This same idea was planted and instilled in her son's mind also from the time he was a little boy.

Years afterwards, Henry McKee suffered severe financial reverses. Rather than sell the slave Robert, as was customary, and see mother and son separated, he gave the boy his permission to go to Charleston to find employment. Mrs. McKee diligently searched for light work for Robert and got him a job as Lamp Lighter on the streets of Charleston, leaving him in the care of her sister, Mrs. Ancrum, who lived there.

Through the years following, Robert worked at several jobs, learning from each. He seemed to have a natural talent where boats were concerned and often was allowed to pilot the craft on which he was employed on its trips between Charleston and Beaufort. Before Robert was eighteen years old, he married Hannah Jones, occasioning great celebration of the marriage rites. The wedding took place in the Mc-Kees' lovely yard in Beaufort, all the guests being served a wedding supper later by the McKee family.

Four years later, war came. Robert Smalls became the pilot of a fast boat known as "The Planter," which transported Confederate troops up and down the coast, and afterwards was the flagship and dispatch boat of General Roswell Ripley, in charge of the defense of Charleston.

To all inquirers who had asked about Robert's responsibility, in every circumstance Henry McKee had answered, "I would trust him anywhere." But one day Henry McKee had occasion to rue this statement, for Robert Smalls had betrayed him and the South. He sailed "The Planter" through the Confederate defenses, giving the well known signals that allowed him to pass, into the Yankee stronghold, surrendering the boat to the Union Army. His temerity was applauded, he was gleefully received, and the former Negro slave began the ascent of the ladder of fame under Yankee tutelage. He became in later years a Republican Congressman from South Carolina, occupying at one time the former McKee home on Prince Street in which he had been a house servant. His last appointment under Federal auspices was a reward for his services to the Yankees, an appointment as Collector of the Port, Beaufort County.

XI

FORT FREDERICK

Beneath the shade of ancient oaks on the grounds of the Naval Hospital, the ruins of Fort Frederick give evidence of the days when Spaniards roved the waters of Beaufort.

Often called "Port Royal's Spanish Fort," its records prove that it was constructed by the British government about 1732. With the passing of time, the tidal waters of Beaufort River have made inroads into the ancient tabby walls of Fort Frederick.

Built on a narrow point between Port Royal and the town of Beaufort, the site was an ideal location for a fortification. Historians claim the "Fort never fired a shot at an enemy vessel," though its thick tabby walls held piercings for guns.

Little is known of the Fort, as its history is lost in the past. But it is a source of much interest to tourists who visit it as a rich example of the art of tabby making.

XII

In 1932—nearly one hundred and seventy-five years after her ancestors came to Beaufort, Miss Eva L. Verdier wrote a small pamphlet entitled "Some Experiences While Taking Census Among the Low Country Negroes of South Carolina."

The following excerpts have been taken from it:

"As I walked along the dusty road with the big book under my arm, I pondered upon these good old colored folk of 'gun shoot' days. Once they were slaves. Now they are masters of their own little one-horse farms."

"When they were freed—they bought small farm plots. Their owners' original plantations were cut up into parcels of land and dealt out to them. It began a new era in their lives. They well remember 'gun shoot' days and by them record their ages.

"The coastal Negro does not date time by Anno Domini, but from events of great excitement or danger. Instead of 'gun shoot' days, the younger ones reckon from the 1886 earthquake, and the still younger ones from the 1893 storm, when over two thousand of them lost their lives in this section."

She wrote on, "These farms are surrounded by salt water creeks from which they get crabs, fish, oysters and shrimp to eat with their 'hominy.'

"One Sunday afternoon I called at this house—knocking and calling were to no avail. I was about to give up when a voice came from a neighboring house, 'Nobody home!' Gratefully I turned in the direction of the voice. It met me at the gate in the person of a young colored youth . . .

" 'Will you please tell me who lives in the house over there?' I inquired. 'One lady libs there Ma'am, but she gone to S'Ciety meetin'.'

"I groaned inwardly. 'One Lady,' . . . all this work and I being paid per person! But I inquired her name.

" 'She name Miss Olivia,' he informed me.

" 'Miss Olivia *what*? Can you give me her last name?'

" 'No, Ma'am, I don't rightly members she trimmins'.'

"I finally located 'Miss Olivia' and secured her trimmins'."

"I used to relate amusing incidents to my wash woman who lives in town. She was much interested and laughed heartily about the boy not knowing 'Miss Olivia's trimmins'.'

" 'Don't know she trimmings,' she said in derision, 'ain't that funny now? Well, you just has to 'scuse country folks, they ain't know any better. Now what he should hab say is, "*I don't know she entitlements*".' "

These are just a few of the incidents Miss Verdier related.

* * * *

Many, many tales are told of old Beaufort. Among them is the thrilling story of the Regiment of "Tall Men" (all six feet or over) who fought in the Confederate War.

At one time, ship building was quite an important industry at Beaufort and on Hilton Head.

Beaufort had a large and rare library until the Confederate War. In 1861 the books were shipped to the North and held as confiscated chattel property.

Beaufort

When the night color slowly drains away,
When the early morning mists rise from the river,
When the swaying Spanish moss reveals itself,
When the Town of Beaufort's houses and church
    spires are discernible,
When low over the water sounds the lonely call
    for oyster shuckers,
When the bridge swings wide for tug or towering
    two-master,
When the shrimpers come in from their night on
    the ocean,
Then all is well—a good fresh day is emerging!

Isabel B. Hoogenboom.

Modern Beaufort

DRIVING along the Bay, through Beaufort's main business section, one may catch a glimpse of the many boats that dock along the river back of the stores.

A tiny row boat may be wedged in between two palatial yachts; sail boats rock gently as their owners wait for the breeze to carry them out on the Bay. But, more often, one will see several shrimp boats refueling, their large black nets hanging from long masts like giant mourning veils.

Shrimping is one of Beaufort's largest industries. From the Chamber of Commerce booklet comes the information that as a result of the county's being a fishing center, other activities spring up, including plants for canning oysters, crabs and shrimp.

Beaufort county's fertile farm lands are capable of producing, with industry, anything requisite for luxurious living. They are especially adapted to trucking and the commercial raising and feeding of cattle.

The Marine Corps Recruit Depot is located at Parris Island, six miles from Beaufort, and the Marine Air Station on Port Royal.

Today, the tourist trade is a considerable item in Beaufort's economy. Many luxurious motels cater to the most fastidious travelers. One of the newer is the "Sea Island." Built on the site of the old hotel of the same name, its handsome brick buildings, decorated with lacy iron work, are reminiscent of other days. Broad pavements have replaced the tall trees and velvety lawns that were enclosed by a handsome iron fence around the old hotel.

Inside, the motel is as modern as a fine architect could plan. But it retains the charm and hospitality that made its namesake famous for fine foods.

One specialty, "Crab Soup," is so delicious that a guest, after being served this gourmet's delight, rarely fails to ask for the recipe. The request is made so often that the management keeps printed copies at the Restaurant's cash register.

GENERAL PATE'S FAMOUS CRAB SOUP
Recommended by *Holiday* Magazine

INGREDIENTS

(For one serving)

⅛ cup of chopped Beaufort crabmeat
3 tablespoons tomato soup
1 tablespoon finely chopped onion
1¾ cups evaporated milk
1 tablespoon butter
1 teaspoon flour
1 teaspoon cooking sherry
1 teaspoon Worcestershire sauce

DIRECTIONS

Saute onion and flour in butter, and add chopped crab meat. Add three (3) tablespoons tomato soup to the crab mixture and heat. Heat the evaporated milk in a separate container. When the milk is hot, remove from the heat and blend into the crab meat and tomato soup mixture. Stir in one (1) tablespoon of cooking sherry and the one (1) teaspoon of Worcestershire sauce. Serve hot in a heated soup bowl.

If a thinner soup is desired, simply add water to the evaporated milk before heating.

* * * * *

Fun and relaxation set the mood for Beaufort. Here one finds an unsurpassed climate; amusement for young and old—dancing, golfing, water skiing, fishing, sailing. Its fame has spread afar—visitors return and new ones come.

A colorful water festival is held in July and a queen of the Carolina Sea Islands is crowned. In August, the equally famous Sailing Regatta takes place; and in September the annual art show.

Many writers come to Beaufort to get material and color for their books. In the present day two of "Beaufort's own" reflect pride on their town. Ann Head has written many delightful stories that have gained popularity over the country. Gracious and talented Chlotilde Martin wrote the text for "Sea Islands to Sand Hills," and has appeared in many newspapers and magazines with her feature articles. Her "Low Country" column, published now for many years by Charleston's *The News and Courier,* is a source of interest and pleasure throughout South Carolina.

But one attraction is gone forever from St. Helena Sound near Beaufort. For a number of years a snow white porpoise —thought to be the only one in the world—was a familiar sight in the bright blue waters. Children loved to watch the great white mammal as it swam and cavorted daily near the shore. They named her "Peaches." Fame brought a sad ending to the little story. The Miami Seaquarium heard of the rare albino porpoise and decided to capture her. Fitting out a ship with the necessary equipment and crew, the Seaquarium sent them to Beaufort waters. Here the crew was informed that it is illegal to trap or molest porpoises in Beaufort County waters. Retreating to Colleton County—accompanied by game wardens and newspaper men—the intruders bided their time. The white porpoise, unaware that her last day of freedom had come, swam gleefully through the smooth waters of St. Helena Sound and across the county line. There she was ensnared in a huge net and carried to Florida where she will remain in captivity. Her one remaining link with her home is that she has been renamed "Carolina Snowball." One wonders if she misses the vast shimmering waters, chasing fish and rolling in play with her kind!

The luxurious rhapsody of plantation life in the golden age, when indigo, rice and cotton brought tremendous wealth to the Sea Islands, is gone forever. But some of the elegant old houses still stand in their walled-in gardens. Only a few are occupied by descendants of the builders.

Automobiles roll over the same narrow, winding, picturesque streets where once fine carriages were driven by Negro coachmen in livery.

Modern Beaufort, just as beautiful as in the past, has become a thriving little city—progressive and enterprising. Yet it retains a strange magic that lures, and lingers in the hearts of visitors and those who have called it home.

Years ago, Robert Woodward Barnwell, Sr., wrote

"Called Back"

I think if I could see once more
The tide at Beaufort sweep,
Just as the crimson fades to gray,
Just as the shadows creep.
Just as the star of evening glows
And the skimming swallows seek repose
There where the oleanders grow
Before my boyhood's home,
Stumbler and groper that I've been,
Panting on the mountain path,
Lost in the forest green,
Wrecked by the Ocean's wrath,
Stifled in throng of men;
Come for the wanderer's rest;
Come to the home loved best. . . .